Drifting Toward

"The Story Five of Japanese; A very Handsome Tails.
Dated Oct. 26, 1852. John Mung."

The English-language title page of *Hyoson Kiryaku* is written by Manjiro and signed using his alias, John Mung. —*Rosenbach Museum & Library*

Drifting Toward the Southeast

The Story of Five Japanese Castaways

A complete translation of

Hyoson Kiryaku

(A Brief Account of Drifting Toward the Southeast)

As told to the court of Lord Yamauchi of Tosa in 1852 by

John Manjiro

Transcribed and illustrated by

Kawada Shoryo

Translated by

Junya Nagakuni and Junji Kitadai

With a Foreword by Stuart M. Frank

Spinner Publications, Inc.

New Bedford, Massachusetts

Translation © 2003 Junya Nagakuni and Junji Kitadai
All rights reserved.
© Spinner Publications, Inc.
New Bedford, Massachusetts 02740
Printed in the United States of America

ISBN 0-932027-59-8 (cloth)
ISBN 0-932027-56-3 (paper)

Library of Congress Cataloging-in-Publication Data

Kawada, Shoryo, 1824-1898.
 [Hyoson kiryaku. English]
 Drifting toward the southeast : the story of five Japanese castaways :
a complete translation of Hyōson kiryaku / transcribed and illustrated
by Kawada Shoryo ; foreword by Stuart M. Frank ; translated by Junya
Nagakuni, and Junji Kitadai.
     p. cm.
 Includes bibliographical references and index.
 ISBN 0-932027-59-8 (pbk. : alk. paper) -- ISBN 0-932027-56-3 (cloth :
alk. paper)
 1. United States--Description and travel. 2. Nakahama, Manjirō,
1827-1898. 3. Japan--History--Restoration, 1853-1870. I. Nagakuni,
Junya, 1939- II. Kitadai, Junji, 1932- III. Title.
E166 .K2513 2004
952'.025'092--dc22

                                        2003021031

Contents

Acknowledgments / Credits

The publishers and translators would like to thank the Rosenbach Museum and Library in Philadelphia, the Millicent Library in Fairhaven, Massachusetts, the Sumiyoshi Shrine in Osaka, Mr. Kiichi Matsuoka of Kochi City, and the Kochi Prefectural Museum of History for the use of their *Hyoson Kiryaku* manuscripts. We are grateful for the support of the Japan Society of Boston, the Consulate-General of Japan in Boston, the Kochi City Library, and the New Bedford Whaling Museum/Kendall Institute.

Translators / Authors

Junya Nagakuni
Junji Kitadai

Editors

Joseph D. Thomas
Junji Kitadai
Marsha L. McCabe

Production

Jay Avila
Andrea V. Tavares
Milton P. George
Cyril Moreno
Derek Ellis
Anne J. Thomas

Grant Support

Acushnet Foundation
Community Foundation of Southeastern
    Massachusetts — Rainy Day Fund
Crapo Foundation
Fairhaven/New Bedford–Tosa Shimizu
    Sister City Committee
Fairhaven Arts Council
Furthermore Foundation
LEF Foundation
Massachusetts Cultural Council

Copy Editors / Proofreaders

Stuart M. Frank
Takiji Tanaka
Takashi Sugita
Dianne Wood
Tamia Burt

Contributors

A & A Seafood, Inc.
Christopher Benfey
Ruth Caswell
Clarence Cross
Tracy A. Furtado
Jim Grasela
Peter Grilli
Judith Guston
Walle Hargreaves
Yasuo Komatsu
Luiz Family of Dartmouth
Charles Momeny
Arthur and Cheryl Moniz
Hiroshi Nakahama
Claire Nemes
Keiten Okamoto
Kikuko Ohno
Peckham Rental Center, Inc.
Gerald and Ayako Rooney
Hayato Sakurai
Yumi Tanaka
Michishige Udaka
Masumi Ueta
Norihiko Yasuoka

Foreword

Manjiro: A Portrait of the Castaway as a Young Man

by Stuart M. Frank, New Bedford Whaling Museum

anjiro was not the only castaway to return to Japan after a protracted sojourn in the West, nor even the first to return brimming with enthusiasm for superior American whaling methods. Nor was he the first to promote the introduction of these methods in Japan. Already, in 1843, the castaway Jirokichi, who had been rescued by the Nantucket whaleship *James Loper* five years earlier, had returned to "that double-bolted land" with news of Yankee whaling, but without result. Jirokichi was evidently not as convincing as Manjiro would be almost a decade later, and the Tokugawa government was not yet ready to listen. Meanwhile, other such castaways who dared trickle in from analogous rescues—those who were not executed or imprisoned—were generally ignored.

Nor was Manjiro the only Japanese who possessed intimate knowledge of potentially useful Western technologies prior to the opening of Japan in 1854. In the mid 19th century, with the blessing and encouragement of the Shogunate and local *daimyos,* who were eager to introduce Western technology, there were a considerable number of scholars studying the Dutch language and Dutch texts in schools in various parts of Japan. One of these was young Yukichi Fukuzawa— the future founder of Keio University in Tokyo— who by 1854 was already reaching across the sea to harvest Western ideas, studying Dutch at Osaka and Nagasaki, first as a student, then as a teacher, then as headmaster and guiding spirit in such schools.

Fukuzawa, along with Manjiro, was a member of the first Japanese diplomatic mission to the West in 1860. He became an avid promoter of American ethics and American technology in Japan—including American whaling methods—and his school of transcription and translation has been called the real cornerstone of Keio University. Early along, by the time of the Treaty of Five Nations (1859), which opened the port of Yokohama to foreign trade (Shimoda, Hakodate, and Nagasaki were already "open" on a limited basis), Fukuzawa had already mastered written Dutch and was rapidly conquering written and spoken English, which he had immediately recognized as the necessary *lingua franca* of learning and trade in the emerging internation-alist environment. He crossed the ocean several times, visiting America and Europe, gained a practical knowledge of several European languages as well as Chinese and Korean, and became a leading light of ethical, intellectual, and methodological advancement in Japan.

No, Manjiro was neither the first nor the only, but his experience and his unique accomplishments went deeper than the others, and his persuasive powers must have been considerable. Moreover, his contributions were unique. Fukuzawa was a theoretician, an admin-istrator, and an intellectual. Manjiro was a sailor, an artisan, and a hands-on practical man. He not only had *been* abroad but had really *lived* abroad for an entire decade during his formative years. He attended school and church in Fairhaven, Massachusetts, lived with an American family in American home-and-hearth style; and was gainfully employed, rewarded, and promoted for his skill in several trades. Moreover, as Junji Kitadai points out in his Epilogue, quoting from *Moby-Dick,* "a whale-ship was [Manjiro's] Yale College and [his] Harvard," as it had been for Melville and for Ishmael. For it was on two voyages at sea, in the *John Howland* as a callow castaway and in the *Franklin* as a mature young professional, that Manjiro received his "degree" in Western ways. His postgraduate education was in the gold fields of California, where he developed the stamina and the resolve to return with his companions to Japan. When he finally did return, it was in a sophisticated Western seagoing craft under his own command. His homecoming was one not of a simple fisherman but of a seasoned practitioner who had succeeded at four practical trades—sailor, whaleman, cooper, and prospector—with skills that would be useful to him later.

As a sailor, he knew enough celestial navigation to teach it and promote its use in Japan, and he was already accustomed to ocean tempests and seasickness. He was thus able to function competently when, in 1860, Japan's first diplomatic mission, of which he was a member, encountered a debilitating gale on the high seas. Whether or not the story be apocryphal of Manjiro having saved the ship through his competence and level-headedness when most others were disabled by the storm, he must have contributed more than his fair share as the only Japanese on board who had actually made a sea voyage—in fact having traversed the Atlantic and crossed the Indian and Pacific oceans several times. His attempts to introduce American whaling methods in two outings of the Japanese schooner *Ichiban-maru* were failures, although evidently not because of any shortfall in Manjiro's seamanship.

As a whaleman, Manjiro had his first, unwitting apprenticeship as a boy aboard the *John Howland.* By the time of the *Franklin* voyage he was already functionally literate in English, had studied navigation, was steeped in the whaling lore of New Bedford and Fairhaven, and had almost two years at sea on the *John Howland* to recommend him. Possibly because of his still-young age, possibly because of lingering racial prejudice, he was shipped out on the *Franklin* as steward—a not inconsiderable post, in any case, as it paid better than a common foremast hand and entailed responsibility for provisions and stores as well as for meals and accommodations in the aftercabin. As steward he would nevertherless have pulled an oar in a whaleboat and been very much a part of the crew.

When the captain fell ill and had to be removed, there followed an inevitable reshuffling of the hierarchy of command. The chief mate advanced to captain, the other mates each moved up a slot, and one of the boatsteerers (harpooners) was promoted to fourth mate—thus creating a vacancy in the responsible, professional post of boatsteerer. In true Yankee fashion, the crew elected the man they most wanted for boatsteerer—a post in which skill, courage, and steadfastness would contribute to their livelihoods and where any lack of skill, courage, and steadfastness would cost them money, risk their lives unnecessarily, and prolong the voyage. The man they chose was Manjiro.[1] While Manjiro did not complete the requisite seven-year apprenticeship to qualify him as a bona fide journeyman cooper, his training in making tight barrels for the whaling trade would have been an advantage in later endeavors. First of all, it familiarized him with a variety of universally useful woodworking tools and methods. Aboard a whaleship the ship's cooper would preside over a thousand or two tight casks that had been built ashore (conceivably by the very cooper under whom Manjiro trained), and then were disassembled and bundled into *shooks* belowdeck, for reassembly when the occasion arose to stow down sperm oil and whale oil.

Aboard the *Franklin*, Manjiro was likely the number two man on barrels and casks, opening them and tracking the contents in his capacity as steward, assisting the cooper assemble barrels from shooks, insuring their watertightness and thus their ability to preserve the precious cargo of oil. As a sailor and worker in wood, Manjiro had the skill and insight to select, equip, and command the whaleboat that would carry him and his companions back to Japan. Most of all, his training and experience as a cooper would have imparted an intimate sense of what was required at the infrastructural level of Yankee whaling, and an appreciation of the grassroots quality of American life that set the standards for the improvements he envisioned for Japan.

Manjiro has been called "The Man Who Discovered America," a transparent allusion to Christopher Columbus. This epithet is more apropos and less cleverly gratuitous than it may superficially appear. Columbus died without realizing that he had made a discovery at all, much less appreciating the magnitude of that discovery. What Columbus found, but failed to realize he found, was not the route to China he expected but a so-called "New World" that no one in Europe knew was there. Manjiro's discovery was of an entirely different order. Japan knew of the existence of the West but had hitherto deliberately ignored it, purposefully shut it out, carefully minimized any contact with it, and unleashed its wrath on any who consorted with it. What Manjiro discovered was not that there *was* an America, but that what there was *in* America might be worthwhile and progressive for Japan.

Thanks to the depth and thoroughness of his experience, and the tenacity and clarity of his character, through patience, persistence, and articulate polemic he was able to accomplish something unique in the Japanese experience. This was not only to save the lives of himself and his companions but to enlighten the intractable Shogunate and enhance Japan's willingness to accept the inevitable foisted upon them by Perry and the West, and to embrace the future as one of promise and potential for the betterment of Japan, including the betterment of working people from humble origins who were tradesmen, sailors, and fishers like himself. Unlike Columbus, who discovered a place but died ignorant of its significance and potential, Manjiro was a visionary who had great expectations for a newly liberated Japan.

1. There has been a persistent misunderstanding of Manjiro's role aboard the *Franklin*. His new position is described in Japanese as *fuku sencho*, meaning "sub-captain" or "deputy captain." In Japan, this has been erroneously interpreted as sub-captain of the *ship*—that is, First Mate of the *Franklin*. (The misinterpretation originated in a biography of Manjiro, entitled *Nakahama Manjiro Den*, written by his eldest son, Toichiro Nakahama, in 1936.) However, such a leap, from steward directly to mate, would have been impossible for so young and comparatively inexperienced a foreign lad, who had completed portions of only two whaling voyages and was hitherto still in the forecastle as a lowly steward, whether or not he may have mastered celestial navigation. Rather, it is clear from the context that Manjiro was promoted to "sub-captain" of his *boat*—that is, as *boatsteerer* (*harpooner*), and as such second in command to the officer in charge of one of the whaleboats. The officer in charge would have been one of the mates or even the new captain.

Preface

by Junya Nagakuni

This translation of the nineteenth-century manuscript *Hyoson Kiryaku (A Brief Account of Drifting Toward the Southeast)*, written by Kawada Shoryo, is the official report of the adventures of five Japanese fishermen shipwrecked off the Province of Tosa, Japan, now known as Kochi Prefecture. It was written at the request of the local court in Tosa that investigated their return after an absence of ten years.

In January 1841, the five fishermen were caught in a sudden storm that whipped their boat out to sea. Drifting southeast, they landed on an uninhabited volcanic island in the Pacific Ocean and struggled to survive. After several months, they were rescued by Captain William H. Whitfield of Fairhaven, Massachusetts, who recorded the event in the navigation log of his ship, *John Howland*.

> *Sunday, June 27*
> *This day light wind from SE. The isle in sight. At 1 PM sent in 2 boats to see if there was any turtle, found 5 poor distressed people on the isle, took them off, could not understand anything from them more than that they were hungry. Made the latitude of the isle 30.*

> *Monday, June 28*
> *This day light winds from SE. The isle land in sight to the westward. [Stayed] to the SW. At 1 PM landed and brought off what few clothes the 5 men left.*

This dramatic encounter was the beginning of the first friendly contact between the Japanese and the American people. Japan had been a closed country for nearly two and a half centuries under the Tokugawa Shogunate, dating from before the Pilgrims landed in Plymouth, Massachusetts, in 1620.

Captain Whitfield took Manjiro and his companions to Oahu, Hawaii, knowing it would be dangerous for them to return to Japan in an American ship. The Japanese government took stern measures against perceived threats of colonialism and Christianity. Those Japanese who had contact with foreigners were regarded as spies or Christians and were often executed.

When Captain Whitfield left Hawaii, he suggested that Manjiro, at age 14 the youngest of the castaways, accompany him to the United States and study there. Whitfield was impressed with Manjiro's intelligence and resourcefulness, and the young man was courageous enough to accept the proposal and live in a culture radically different from his own.

Manjiro moved into Whitfield's home in the whaling town of Fairhaven, went to school, and worked part-time like an ordinary American boy. During his ten years living outside

Japan, he learned English, navigation, and cooperage; he became a competent sailor, a skilled whaler, and a forty-niner who struck gold in the California gold rush. These were amazing adventures and intellectual experiences for a boy who had grown up in a poor fishing village in feudal Japan.

When Manjiro and two other castaways, Denzo and Goemon, returned to Japan in 1851, they were arrested. It was illegal for castaways to return to Japan according to the laws of seclusion. A gruelling series of interrogations followed. Eventually, they were sent to Nagasaki and put in confinement for further questioning for another ten months.

During a final interrogation in Kochi, which lasted 70 days, officials found it dif-

Capt. Whitfield's Sconticut Neck Home

In May 1843, immediately after the widower Whitfield remarried, the newlyweds purchased a 14-acre farm with farmhouse on Sconticut Neck in Fairhaven. Here Manjiro learned to farm and tend animals. Abutting the property was the Sconticut Neck School House, a rickety, one-room shed that Manjiro attended with about 20 other students. (See Appendix.) —*Millicent Library*

ficult to understand their story, as most of what they described about their lives overseas was alien to the insular officials. To facilitate understanding, the prominent samurai artist and scholar Kawada Shoryo was assigned to transcribe and illustrate the account. Shoryo had learned Dutch in Nagasaki and was well known for his knowledge of the outside world as well as for his artistic skills. Especially interested in Manjiro, he obtained permission from the officials to bring Manjiro to his own home where they lived together while Shoryo gathered more information. Shoryo, 27, and Manjiro, 25, formed a close rapport. In an interesting collaboration between a scholar/artist and an American-educated castaway, Shoryo helped Manjiro brush up on his Japanese while Manjiro taught him English.

Shoryo recorded the castaways' testimony in detailed brush-written calligraphy and delicate watercolor illustrations. He bound the document into a four-volume set and named it *Hyoson Kirykau*, literally "A Brief Account of Drifting Toward the Southeast," and presented the finished work to Lord Yamauchi of Tosa, the ruler of the domain, in the autumn of 1852. Manjiro himself wrote the title page: "The Story Five of Japanese. A Very Handsome Tail. October 25, 1852." The short, enigmatic English phrases might well suggest the dilemma of a man trying to describe an unimaginable adventure too fantastic to be described in words.

Hyoson Kiryaku is a significant historical account which Shoryo took pains not to embellish. Shoryo's pictorial rendering, with the help of Manjiro's own sketches, added a unique flavor to the manuscript. It was Japan's first glimpse of America, Yankee-style whaling, and exotic life in the South Pacific.

At the time, the Tokugawa Shogunate and the Japanese policymakers were aware of the imminent threat that the Western powers posed to the island empire. Coincidentally, *Hyoson Kiryaku* was completed just nine months before Commodore Matthew Perry's

Nakahama Manjiro

Born in 1827, Manjiro was one of five children of the fisherman Etsuske, and his wife Shio. This photograph of Manjiro was made around 1880. *Millicent Library*

Kawada Shoryo

Born in Kochi in 1824, Shoryo studied in Edo [Tokyo], Kyoto, Osaka and Nagasaki, and became an accomplished painter and scholar. This self-portrait may be the only known likeness of the man. *Michishige Udaka*

Captain Wm. H. Whitfield

Captain Whitfield, seen here at about age 60, began his maritime career as a 15-year-old crewman aboard the New Bedford whaleship *Martha* in 1819. *Millicent Library*

"Black Ships" armada strong-armed Japan into a peace treaty. *Hyoson Kiryaku* became coveted reading of daimyos and samurai leaders. As a result, numerous hand-written copies circulated, and the castaways' story spread by word of mouth. It caught the imagination of the common people, who were eager to know about the outside world, and shaped their perceptions of mid-nineteenth century America.

Forced to open Japan's borders, the Tokugawa Shogunate government began to realize that Manjiro could be useful for his knowledge of English and Western culture. He served as a secretary to the central Tokugawa government, and he achieved samurai status, which was a remarkable feat for a fisherman from a poor family.

Soon after the Meiji Restoration, Manjiro was dispatched to Europe and to the United States, where he was able to visit Captain Whitfield, taking a train from New York to Fairhaven. He was 43 years old and Captain Whitfield was 65 when they met again. Manjiro slept in his old room in the home at Sconticut Neck.

A statue of Manjiro, holding an octant in one hand and facing the Pacific, stands at Cape Ashizuri near his birthplace in Kochi Prefecture. The statue is modeled after a picture taken when Manjiro was a professor at Tokyo Imperial University. Manjiro died on November 12, 1898, in Tokyo.

When we Japanese talk about the beginning of the modernization of Japan, Nakahama Manjiro and Sakamoto Ryoma always come to mind. The latter is a major figure in the Meiji Restoration and in the birth of democracy in Japan. He was born and raised in Kochi and is said to have been introduced to the idea of democracy by *Hyoson Kiryaku*.

In spite of its popularity, the original manuscript and its copies were lost for many years. In 1912, Stewart Culin, curator of the Brooklyn Museum, was visiting a book fair in Tokyo and "discovered" four volumes of an old Japanese manuscript with quaint colored illustrations, one of which resembled a New England scene. He bought the manuscript and showed it to Dr. Toichiro Nakahama, the first son of Manjiro, who verified the manuscript to be *Hyoson Kiryaku*. It was believed to be a complete copy of the original.

With Culin's consent, Dr. Nakahama made a hand-drawn copy of the manuscript, which is still in the possession of the Nakahama family. A second copy was made from the Nakahama copy and presented to the Millicent Library of Fairhaven in 1920. After Culin's death, his copy was sold to an American book collector and in 1966 it was bought by the Rosenbach Museum and Library in Philadelphia. In Japan, seven copies of *Hyoson Kiryaku* have surfaced, but none has been positively identified as the original.

For this translation, the Rosenbach copy serves as the original text and source of most of the illustrations. We have also used illustrations, believed to be from the hand of Shoryo, taken from the copies kept by the Sumiyoshi Shrine in Osaka and by Mr. Kiichi Matsuoka in Kochi. Some illustrations are from another *Hyoson Kiryaku* found by Mr. Yamaji Kishi in Osaka and currently kept by the Kochi Prefectural Museum of History.

One of the unique features of *Hyoson Kiryaku* is the way Shoryo, who had no knowledge of English, phonetically transcribed English words into *katakana* (as he meticulously explains in the Transcriber's Notes). Katakana shows how the castaways pronounced English words and, more precisely, how their pronunciation sounded to Shoryo. For example, "New Bedford" is transcribed in katakana as "ヌーベッホー" or "Nū Behhō." In our translation, in order to keep the flavor of the original text, we occasionally show Shoryo's katakana pronunciation in brackets following the English translation, for example, "North America [Nosu Merike]."

In the Appendix, we provide a general explanation of the language systems used in *Hyoson Kiryaku* as well as a brief description of the the lunar calendar and the twelve horary signs used to denote time and direction.

Lastly, in our translation, for all the historical Japanese figures, we use the customary Japanese method of placing a person's family name before his or her given name, as in "Kawada Shoryo" and "Nakahama Manjiro."

THE MORNING MERCURY, THURSDAY,

MANUSCRIPTS OF NAKAHAMA DISCOVERED BY STEWART CULIN

Curator of Brooklyn Museum Found Them in Tokyo, with Quaint Illustrations Drawn by Nakahama of Old Fairhaven Drawbridge, Capt. Whitfield's Cow, and Other Objects Strange to the Japanese.

Hyoson Kiryaku Discovered

On July 4, 1918, the *Morning Mercury* of New Bedford carried this article written by Stewart Culin, describing his serendipitous find.

Hyoson Kiryaku

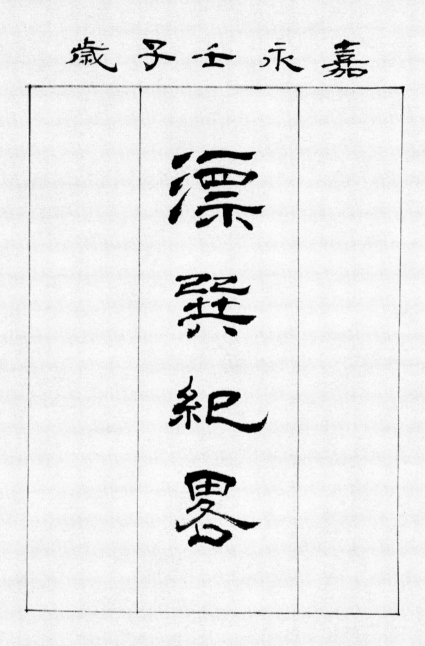

"A Brief Account of Drifting Toward the Southeast, 1852"

The title page of *Hyoson Kiryaku* begins with five small characters at the top which read, from right to left, "Kaei Mizunoe-ne No Toshi," and tell us that this is the Year of the Rat, the fifth year of Kaei [1852]. The large characters written vertically at center give us the title, "Hyo [Drifting] Son [Southeast] Ki [Account] Ryaku [Brief]." *Rosenbach Museum & Library*

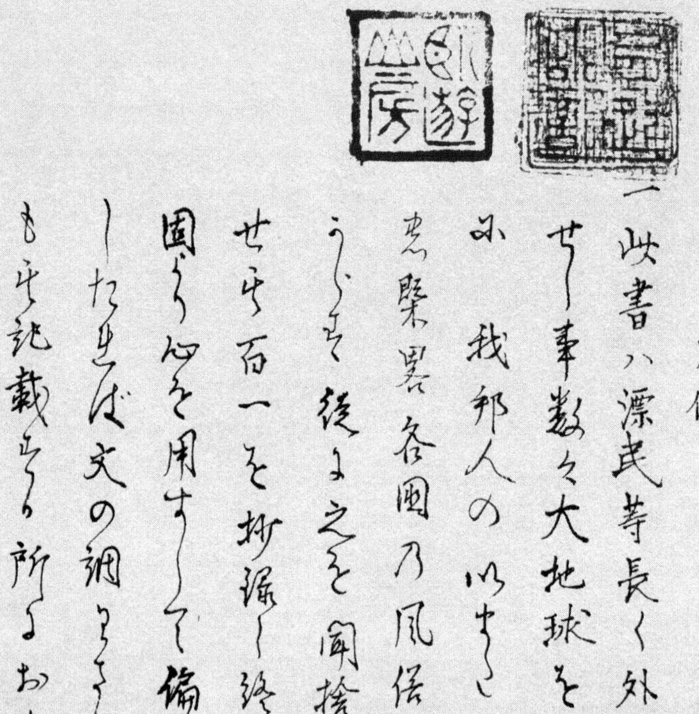

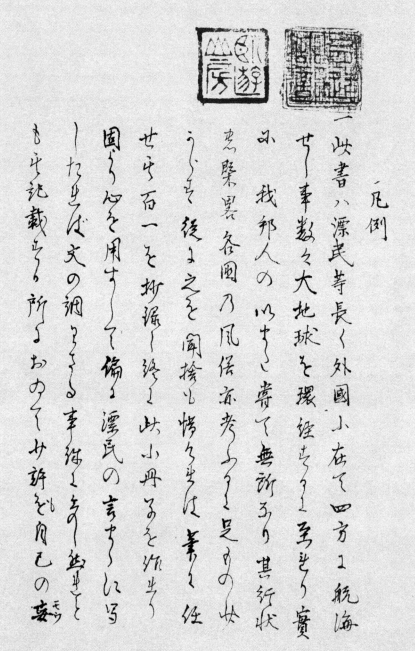

Page One

The two box signature seals in red ink are typically the author's seal. The first symbol (far right) is illegible. The second, pronounced *gwa yu san bo,* indicates that the artist is at ease in his mountain retreat. Neither of these symbols has ever been attributed to Kawada Shoryo, the author of *Hyoson Kiryaku.* They may belong to the one-time owner of the Rosenbach manuscript. *Rosenbach Museum & Library*

Transcriber's Notes

This book tells the story of five Japanese castaways who made lengthy stays in foreign countries and sailed the seas in all directions, circumnavigating the globe several times. Indeed, no Japanese has ever accomplished such a feat. The castaways' knowledge of foreign customs and manners is of great value, and it would be a regrettable loss not to record their experiences. Therefore, I tried to transcribe all the stories they had to tell, but this account is but a hundredth of their whole story. I tried to record all their words faithfully. As such, there may be many awkward wordings in expression, but nowhere in the book have I added my own observations.

Katakana is inserted into the *hiragana* sentences in order to transcribe foreign words and some Japanese words which do not have equivalent *kanji*.[1] Those katakana words are put in parentheses in order to distinguish them from other words.

Contracted sounds like *cha* (チャ), *kya* (キャ), *aeo* (ァオ), or *aeme* (ェメ) are transcribed using two katakana letters, one of them in smaller form. The two letters are to be pronounced together, but the smaller receives less emphasis in sound.

Though many Western names have been transcribed phonetically into kanji by the Chinese, in many instances they do not correspond to what the castaways pronounced. In these cases, katakana is used. In cases where equivalent Chinese characters can be found, katakana is accompanied by small kanji on the side, such as シャンフチ 散土微私 (Sandwich) and ノヲスメリケ 北米利堅 (North America). This is for the benefit of readers who understand Chinese characters. Commonly used kanji names are accompanied by katakana so that readers can make a comparison, such as 日本 ジャパン (Japan) and 漢土 チァィニ (China).

The illustrations and drawings that appear in the book were first drawn by Manjiro, then revised and finished by me after studying foreign books. The drawings with autographs of John Mung were original sketches by Manjiro and no changes were added.

Map Legend

• The greenish-blue line indicates the course the five fishermen drifted during the storm, arriving on an uninhabited island in January of the Year of the Ox [1841]. It is also the course taken by the American ship that rescued them and took them to Oahu in October of the same year.

---

1. Around the 9th century, the Japanese developed a writing system based on syllables: *hiragana* and *katakana* (together: *kana*). Of the two kana systems, *hiragana* is more cursive while *katakana* characters are more angular. *Hiragana* is usually only used for spelling Japanese words. It is used in conjuction with *kanji* (Chinese characters first imported to Japan in the 5th century via Korea) to form complete Japanese sentences. Foreign words are spelled with *katakana*. For more information about the kana system of transcription and Japanese writing, see the Appendix.
2. All parentheses used in this text belong to the transcriber, Shoryo. Editorial comments appear in square brackets.

- The magenta line indicates the course Manjiro took on Captain Whitfield's ship, which sailed from Oahu in December of 1841. At this time, Manjiro had parted from the other four castaways. He went on to the Kingsmill Islands [Kiribati] in March in the Year of the Tiger [1842], and stayed in Gyuan [Guam]. They also passed the uninhabited island the castaways had once inhabited, went whaling in the sea south of Japan, and returned to Oahu in August but could not enter the port due to an opposing wind. Manjiro stayed in Eimeo [currently Moorea] in November, and passed the tip of South America in April of the Year of the Rabbit [1843]. Captain Whitfield's ship reached New Bedford, North America, in June.
- The orange line indicates the course Denzo and Goemon took apart from Manjiro. Asking a whaleship captain to employ them so they could return to Japan, they sailed out of Oahu in October of the Year of the Horse [1846]. The two stayed in Guam in January of the Year of the Sheep [1847], then went to Hachijo Island in March. They hoped to land on Hachijo and then return home, but it was too dangerous to land because of the opposing wind. They instead went to Ezo [Hokkaido] to land but could not disembark because the captain would not give his permission. Finally, they headed for the Russian seas and returned to Oahu in October.
- The navy blue line indicates the course Manjiro sailed on out of New Bedford in October of 1846. He traveled through Boston, the Western Islands [Azores Islands], Cape Verde, etc., then passed by Africa, and went on to Timor in February of 1847 and stopped at New Ireland. In March Manjiro dropped anchor at Guam and in April he stopped at the Bonin [Ogasawara] Islands and Manpigoshin

Map Legend

Regarding the maps, Shoryo wrote, "All the names of places visited by the castaways are recorded as they were remembered and pronounced by the castaways. Written in red beside those pronunciations are the Dutch translations used today [1852] in order to help readers understand which names correspond with which places." *Rosenbach Museum & Library* [in Ryukyu Islands]. Then his ship passed by the uninhabited island [Tori Shima or Hurricane Island], sailed the sea south of Japan, and in October arrived in Oahu. In February of the Year of the Monkey [1848], Manjiro stopped in Guam again. He reached Luzon, passed by the sea south of Japan, and visited Guam for the third time in October. In November, his ship passed by the sea off New Ireland, and in February of the Year of the Hen [1849], it stopped at Ceram [in Molucca], then Timor, and other ports. Finally, the ship passed by Africa in May and returned to New Bedford in June.

- The brown line indicates the course Manjiro sailed on out of New Bedford in October of 1849. Manjiro landed in Valparaiso [Chile] in April of the Year of the Dog [1850], then reached California in May, at which time he began gold mining. He left California in August, reached Oahu in September, and sailed out of Oahu in October on a commercial ship with Denzo and Goemon. The castaways landed on Loochoo [Ryukyu Islands] in January of the Year of the Boar [1851] and at long last achieved their aim of returning to Japan.

— Written by Shoryo-shoshi[3] on a winter's day in
the 5th year of Kaei, the Year of the Rat [1852]

3. Shoryo had more than a dozen pen names that he used selectively on different occasions. In *Hyoson Kiryaku,* he refers to himself as Koretazu, Shoryo-shoshi, Shoryoshi, and Hanposai as well as Shoryo.

World Map

The three panels of the world map (opposite page and below) outlining the castaways' voyages are from the Sumiyoshi Shrine's edition of *Hyoson Kiryaku.* Similar world maps from the Rosenbach edition appear an pages 20 and 21.

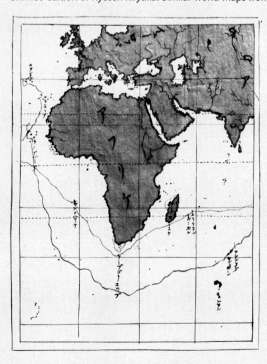
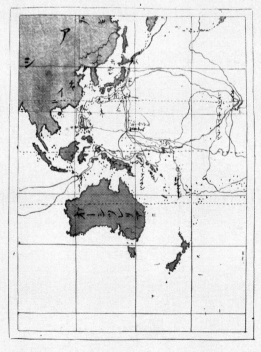

World Map with Routes of the Castaways

Shoryo wrote: "Among the implements the castaways brought back with them was a world map, which Manjiro used to explain where they had been, what the different places were like, and other facts about the world." Of all the maps drawn in the various versions of *Hyoson Kiryaku*, these illustrations from the Rosenbach edition are the most detailed.

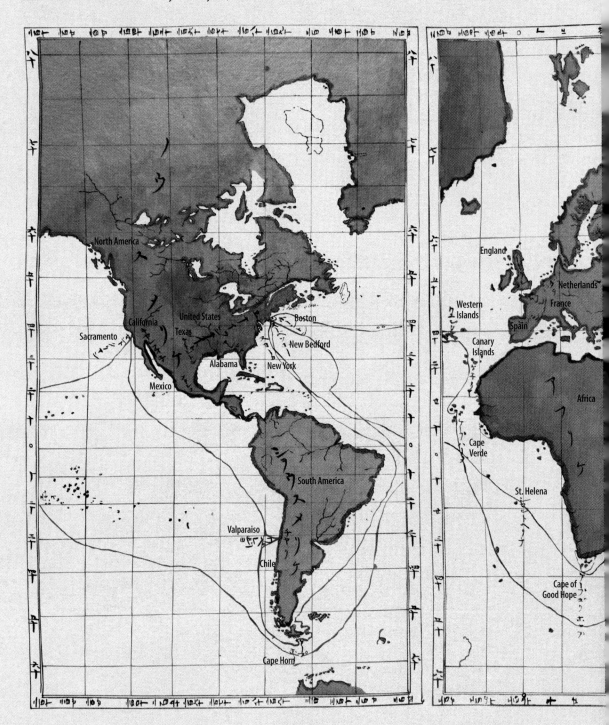

Manjiro's world map is a Mercator projection, a method developed by Flemish geographer Gerardus Mercator (1512–1594) and first used in his world map of 1568. In a Mercator projection, the round earth is rendered on a flat surface. The earth is printed as a rectangle where the meridians and parallels of latitude appear as lines crossing at right angles. Lines are drawn with increasing separation as their distance from the equator increases, and areas appear disproportionately larger the farther they are from the equator, thus distorting the scales. *Rosenbach Museum & Library*

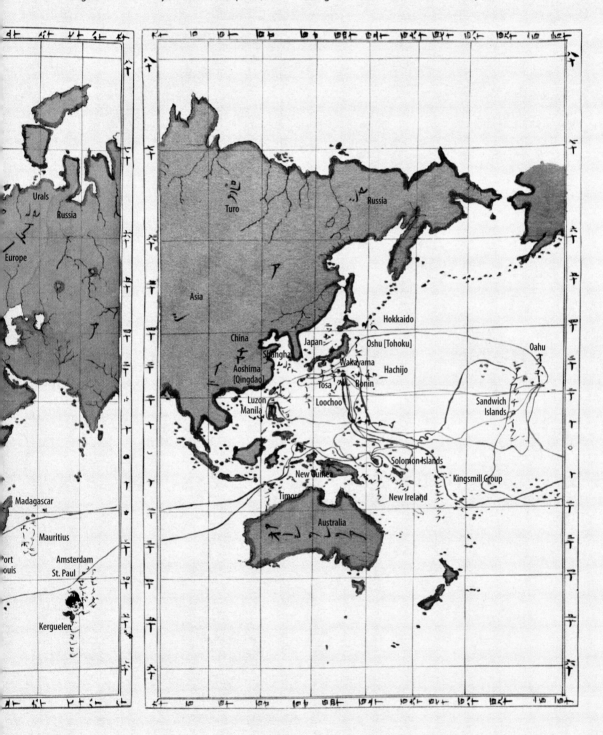

漂巽紀畧卷之一

川田維鶴 撰

小梁子曰　我日本之为邦坤輿中之一海
島也自神皇開基日降仁政德治百穀豐
肥非洋外諸州之可比倫也故航客为黑凡
漂墮外国者亦無不慕舊以歸朝矣本州漂
民傳藏荸以天保辛巳至無人島及撒土微
私北米利幹語壺日夜勞苦計歸朝之事十
数年于兹今兹嘉永壬子遂得其志豈外吾
所謂慕舊也者载亦可以觀我皇囯之美

Book One Summary

Each of the four volumes of *Hyoson Kiryaku* is prefaced with a short paragraph or phrase written in
Chinese that summarizes it. In Book One, Shoryo provides this comparatively lengthy, signed summary,
translated at right. *Rosenbach Museum & Library*

Book One

Shoryo says, "Though Japan is nothing but an island in the world, a benevolent rule has been conducted since the Emperor Jinmu founded the country. No other foreign country can compare with Japan in terms of the abundance of grains grown. Therefore, there is none among those Japanese who were wrecked abroad and drifted to a foreign country that did not yearn for their native traditions and to return home. Denzo and the other Japanese castaways were washed upon an uninhabited island in the Year of the Ox of Tempo. They journeyed to the Sandwich Islands, North America, and other foreign lands, suffering many hardships and toiling day and night. For more than ten years they attempted to return to Japan, and finally fulfilled their wish in the Year of the Rat of Kaei. They are indeed what I call people who yearn after the country and its origins."[1]

— Kawada Koretazu [Shoryo]

---

1. In this peculiar style of quoting himself, Shoryo becomes a third person, or observer, whose observation is merely a brief interjection to the remarkable firsthand account that follows.

*I*n the twelfth year of Tempo, the Year of the Ox[2] [1841], five fishermen set out to fish in the nearby sea. Four of the young Japanese men were from Nishihama, Usa-ura Village in Takaoka County, Province of Tosa [Kochi Prefecture]. They were Fudenojo, 38, his brothers Jusuke, 25, and Goemon, 16, and their neighbor Toraemon, 26. The fifth, Manjiro, 15, was from Nakanohama Village in Hata County.[3] They borrowed a small boat about 24 feet long, owned by a man named Tokuemon at Usa, and loaded it with one-and-a-half bushels of rice, firewood, water and kindling. Sailing from Usa-ura harbor at about ten on the morning of the fifth day of January, they headed west and weighed in overnight at Nishigakari, Yozu, with other boats similar to theirs.

On the sixth day of the month they reached the fishing ground called the Nawaba-nada, about 15 miles off Saga Village, and caught 14 or 15 small fish. That night they stayed at Shirahama, Inomisaki, and cooked some of their fish for dinner. Early on the morning of the seventh day, they sailed west from Kubotsu-nada to an area about 12 miles off Sada-yama. This was the fishing ground called *shi*, which fellow fishermen also called *Hajikari-nada*. Here a channel runs many miles along the ocean floor and is filled with many varieties of fish. Although the nearby fishing boats quickly headed for this spot, Fudenojo's boat had to proceed cautiously because the crew was young and had limited skills. Finally, after sailing about 25 miles from the other boats, they let out their trawl lines and caught a great many horse mackerel.

At about ten o'clock in the morning the wind shifted, blowing strong out of the southwest. The clouds moved swiftly overhead. Seeing this, the other boats quickly unfurled their sails and headed toward Nuno-zaki. Fudenojo ordered the crew to haul in the fishing gear and set sail for land—about 18 miles away.

By noon the wind dropped, the clouds stopped, and the sea became calm. Using this opportunity, the men took out their fishing gear and cast their trawls into the sea. Some time later a northwesterly wind began to blow forcefully and the surrounding skies looked threatening. The men quickly pulled in their lines and began sculling frantically. Working together, they raced toward land. As the sun set, waves splashed and sprayed all around them, making it impossible to see ahead. Then a northeasterly wind rose and the two wind currents fought against each other, threatening to overturn the boat several times.

Soon the situation grew desperate as the oarlock for the sculling oar broke off. They tried to fix it by cutting off a section of the gunwale with an axe and fastenening the oar with straw rope. But then the handle of the scull broke in half and the blade was swept away. Now, nothing could be done.

Exhausted, overwhelmed with fatigue, they were at a loss. Fudenojo raised the yard and unfurled the corner of the sail, but the waves crashed into the boat from behind. Though

---

2. For more on the Japanese calendar system, see Appendix.
3. In Japan, as in many countries, a person is "age one" at the time of birth. Therefore, by Western standards the castaways were actually one year younger than determined here.

高岡郡
宇佐浦
傳藏

歳十五

"Denzo of Usa Village,
Takaoka County, Age 50"

傳藏
弟
五右衛門

二十八歳

"Goemon, Denzo's
Younger Brother, Age 28"

This is how the castaways looked after returning to Kochi at the conclusion of the investigation. The men were given Japanese clothes and for the first time since their return, their foreheads were shaved in the traditional Japanese style. Originally named Fudenojo, Denzo changed his name in Hawaii because people there had so much trouble pronouncing Fudenojo. *Rosenbach Museum & Library*

"Manjiro of Nakanohama Village,
Hata County, Age 27"

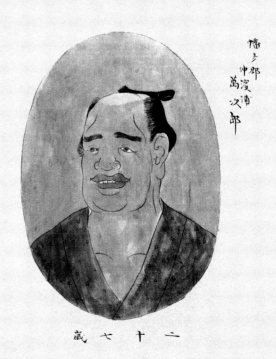

幡多郡
中濱浦
萬次郎

二十七歳

everyone was devoted to his duty, the wind became stronger and the temperatures grew colder. They were freezing, and only Fudenojo held the helm. The boat was swept swiftly like an arrow in a southeast direction. They drifted into the night.

When the next day dawned, the eighth of January, they could see houses on land at Cape Muroto in the morning light. Because these were whaling grounds, the inhabitants had set up a hut at a mountain crest. The crew hoped that a whale spotter in the hut would see them and arrange for their rescue, but their hope was futile. During the commotion the night before, all of the oars had been lost, and they had no way to approach land. As they passed Cape Muroto, the mountains in Kii faded from sight. At the mercy of wind and waves, they drifted far into the ocean. Their only hope was to pray to the gods and Buddha for protection.

On the morning of the ninth, the winds blew from the northwest. On the early morning of the tenth, the winds shifted in their favor and rain began to fall. They covered their boat with rush matting, split wood, prepared some gruel and ate it with fish. Then the rain turned to sleet and they gathered it in their palms and satisfied their thirst. Now the wind shifted to the west again with a rapid current running from the northwest to the southeast. Carried by the current, the vessel flew.

On the eleventh and twelfth, the northwest wind continued to push them toward the southeast. Around noon on the thirteenth day, they caught a dim view of a small island in the southeast direction. Their provisions exhausted, they were unbearably hungry and thirsty. They felt hopeless. If what they saw ahead were truly an island, they would go ashore to obtain water, take an ample sip, and willingly throw themselves into the sea to end their

---

Path of the "Drifters"

This edited section of two maps of Japan that appear on pages 72–73, shows the circuitous path of the drifters from their home port in Tosa, to Hurricane Island, at lower right. *Rosenbach Museum & Library*

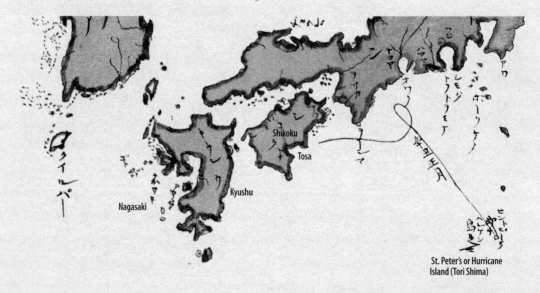

misery. They got to their feet and began to unfurl a substitute corner sail. The wind from the west pushed the boat against a strong current running from the east, causing it to founder, almost capsizing, as it slowly headed toward the island.

By nightfall they neared the north side of the island, but great, craggy rocks made it impossible to approach. To navigate, they tied together the broken pieces of the oar with straw rope and sculled around the island. Soon they came upon a flat beach and dropped anchor about an eighth mile offshore. At this time the wind had died down and the crew assembled at the stern and waited for dawn. They fished, scooped water from the sails, and talked over what to do next—just as they had done the night before.

At dawn on the fourteenth of January they caught several beach fish that were abundant and ate them before noon. Now the time had come for them to throw away their lives. The anchor line was cut, and Toraemon, Goemon, and Manjiro jumped into the sea. Fudenojo and Jusuke were about to follow suit when the boat capsized, and they almost drowned beneath it. The surging waves righted the boat and the brothers managed to swim to a boulder. When they looked back the boat had been dashed to pieces and splinters were scattered among the waves. In the mayhem Jusuke broke his leg and nearly fainted from the severe pain. Toraemon and the others had already gone ashore and shouted for the two brothers. Encouraged, Jusuke was able to swim ashore gradually with his brother beside him.

Once everyone was ashore, some of the men walked around the island to find out its shape. It was a large craggy island about two and a half miles in diameter. Though oleaster [a type of olive tree] and cogon grasses [thatching reed] grew luxuriantly, other shrubs were small and none more than five feet tall. Looking around for something to satisfy their hunger, they found some sprouting Japanese knotweeds. Though they were edible they grew on top of a wall of rock and were unreachable. Walking in a southwest direction they found numerous large and small birds; one group of birds, about 2,000 in number, called *tokuro* [albatross], had built their nests on rocks and were raising their young.

A cave gaped nearby. The castaways crept in on their bellies to find that the cave was about 9 by 15 feet square. The hungry crew ate some birds and took shelter in the cave. Day to day they wondered how to sustain themselves. They made a place to sleep by using pieces of ships' timber that had washed ashore, laying them side by-side. To capture the birds the men raided the nests with sticks. After skinning them with fish spears, they pounded the meat with a handy stone and spread the paste on a sunny rock and baked it. They called it "stone roast" and divided it up every day. In this way more than a hundred days passed. For 60 to 70 of those days no rain fell, not a drop of water even in the crevices of rocks. Now at the end of their resources, the men collected their urine with the palms of their hands and sipped it. However, as there was little water in it, it was insufficient to restore energy, which caused the greatest suffering.

One day Fudenojo, accompanied by Manjiro, set off in search of food and water. Clambering rugged steep rocks, they reached the top and found a large open space where they could walk freely. They came upon several oblong stone structures a few feet in length, and they also found an old well with dirty water at the bottom. Nearby there appeared to be two old graves. Fudenojo thought they were the graves of people who, like them, had washed ashore and lived on the island. They had been buried there. Wondering what was in store for them, Fudenojo was overcome. He chanted the name of Amitabha [Buddha of Infinite Light], wiping his tears with his sleeve. They retraced their steps over the rugged rocks and returned to the cave, telling the others what they had seen. They all broke down in tears at the thought that visitors would one day visit the island and shed tears upon learning that they, too, had starved to death.

"Uninhabited Island"

"The east side of the uninhabited island. Seen from a ship, birds are swarming over the island so thickly that in the extreme case the outline of the island becomes hardly discernible." — *Rosenbach Museum & Library*

"Uninhabited Island" [Tori Shima or Hurricane Island]

The two versions of Hurricane Island [here and facing page] come from two different manuscripts, though they have the same caption. The drawing at left is from the Rosenbach Museum and Library and bears Manjiro's signature. The painting below is from the Sumiyoshi Shrine manuscript and appears to have been made by Shoryo or his transcribers.

Tori Shima, meaning "bird Island" in Japanese, belongs to the Izu island group and is situated about 370 miles south of Tokyo. Because the volcano is still active and dangerous, Tori Shima is uninhabited today. It serves as a breeding ground to the endangered short-tailed albatross. *— Sumiyoshi Shrine*

One day in late April an earthquake struck the island. At night it became more severe, and the cave rocked and rumbled violently. Sand and stones fell around them. When they tried to escape, many great rocks crashed at the entrance of the cave. The castaways huddled together, afraid this was the end. When the earthquake subsided and day broke they saw that a huge rock had obstructed the mouth of the cave. In spite of their terror they were surprised that they had survived the night and they rejoiced over their good luck. The men thought Heaven had thus taken pity on them, they were not forsaken. They prayed that they might have more good luck some day. They pushed away the rock and stepped out.

In early June, at the time of the new moon, finding it hard to sleep, Goemon got up at dawn and looked over the vast sea. He saw something tiny in the southeast. He imagined it was a mountain or a cloud, but after a long while he saw it move. Convinced it was a ship, he quickly woke up the other four to tell them what he had seen. He said that one day in March he had risen early and saw what appeared to be a foreign ship coming from the east and turning north. On this day the shadowy thing they espied was surely a sailing ship like he had seen before. The four men shook their heads and did not believe him. As the ship gradually approached and was about seven miles away, they could tell for certain it was a huge foreign ship. Delighted that luck was with them, they praised Goemon's great wisdom. Unfortunately, it soon became clear that the ship was not approaching the island but heading toward the northwest, too far off to catch a signal.

Discouraged, Toraemon and the others returned to the cave, crying. They did nothing but sigh. At that time, not only did they suffer from lack of water, but the birds had left the island with their young. Though fish were abundant, they had used up their hooks and spears in skinning birds. They collected seaweed and shellfish, partly assuaging their hunger. Then something extraordinary happened.

One day while Manjiro was gathering shellfish on the shore, he saw two boats being lowered from a foreign ship and heading for the island with sails unfurled. He cried out to his mates, "Rescuers! Rescuers! The rescue boats are coming!" Hearing this, Toraemon and Goemon ran forward and tied Goemon's trousers to a broken sail yard, holding them up as a distress signal. The crewmen raised their hats in response.

The boats got closer; each had a six-man crew. The men had long unkempt hair; among them were curly-headed black men. The castaways later learned the boats had come to catch the abundant fish in the sea around the island, not to rescue them. The stranded people took the sailors by surprise. When they saw Toraemon and the two others, they beckoned them to get into the boats. Though the castaways were terrified, not knowing who these strange people were, they took off their clothes and swam to the boats. Asked by the foreigners if there were others, they pointed to the cave and answered them with a gesture indicating: "Two more over there!" The black men from one of the boats ran toward the cave.

Meanwhile, Jusuke's severely injured leg still had not healed. He spent his days lying on the floor of the cave and lived on what the others brought back. Though Fudenojo was so weakened from starvation that he could not walk freely himself, he spent his time caring for

"Complete Map of the Uninhabited Island"

"Latitude N. 31º. Americans call this Hurricane Island *[Hareken Airanto]*. Its circumference is about one ri [2.5 miles]." — *Rosenbach Museum & Library*

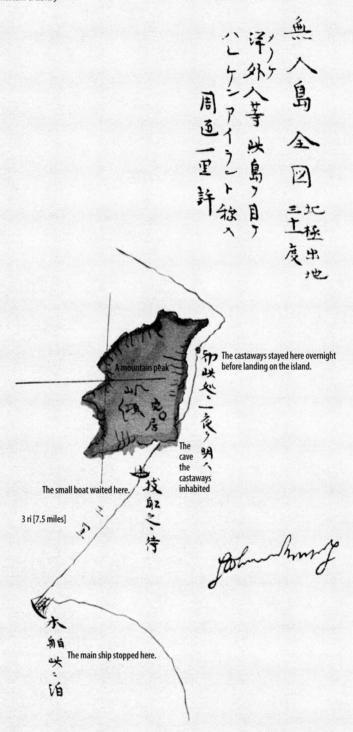

The castaways stayed here overnight before landing on the island.

A mountain peak

The cave the castaways inhabited

The small boat waited here.

3 ri [7.5 miles]

The main ship stopped here.

Jusuke. Just as they were wondering what happened to their crewmates, two strange men, as black as if painted with kettle soot, came to the mouth of the cave. They spoke, but neither castaway knew what the strangers said. They took hold of Fudenojo and tried to lift him. He was so frightened he tried to break free, but they would not let him go. With a gesture, one of the men conveyed that the other three castaways had already been helped onto their boats. Fudenojo understood for the first time they were trying to help. With the men's assistance, Fudenojo limped and his brother Jusuke crawled from the cave to the beach and into the water, swimming toward the small boat. A rope was thrown out to them; they grabbed it and were pulled aboard. The crew then rowed over to the big ship.

As they approached the ship and looked up, Fudenojo and the others were aghast—bewildered by this sudden rescue and halfway between sleeping and waking. The ship was about 180 feet long [30 ken] and 36 feet wide [6 ken], with three masts and eight small boats on deck.[4] Rope ladders were stretched in all directions like a spider's web. With tens of white sails hanging on the ropes, fluttering in the wind, it was quite a spectacle. The foreigners helped them aboard.

They were brought inside the ship to the captain's quarters. Here they saw a row of rooms furnished gorgeously enough to serve as a small shrine for Buddha. The rooms looked so dignified that the castaways were awed and could hardly approach them. They knelt in fear before the captain and his mates. The captain told Fudenojo and the others to come close and said something incomprehensible. Imagining they were being asked what nationality they were, they answered "Nihonjin, Nihonjin." Taking pity on their cold and hunger, the captain took out five suits of dry clothes and showed them by gestures how to wear them.

The cook brought them some steamed sweet potatoes, which the captain disapproved of. Perhaps he thought it unwise for the five men to suddenly eat a lot of food when they had lived so long on the island in a state of starvation. He took back their food and gave them bowls of herb soup and a little pork. Thereafter, the captain gave them solid food gradually. In the morning and evening they were fed hardtack [arete]. For lunch, the crew seemed to eat another kind of food while the five men were served good rice, the captain perhaps guessing they were Japanese. They appreciated the captain's consideration and enjoyed the meals.

This big ship was a whaleship from New Bedford, Massachusetts, from the United States in North America. On board were 6,000 oil barrels, several cows and hogs, grain, two cannons and 30 bayonets. It was manned by 34 men and was called the John James Howland.[5] The captain was William H. Whitfield, a native of Fairhaven, a town bordering New Bedford. He was about 40 years old, fair of skin, jet-black hair trimmed and combed straight back,

4. The actual dimensions of the New Bedford ship John Howland at the time of Manjiro's rescue were length 111 feet 10 inches, breadth 27 feet 5 inches, depth 13 feet 8½ inches; and volume 376.86 register tons.
5. Manjiro repeatedly misnamed the ship John James Howland, though it was simply named John Howland. Owned by brothers John and James Howland, she was named after their father and constructed at New Bedford in 1830 by Jethro & Zachariah Hillman—the same shipbuilder brothers who built the Charles W. Morgan in 1841. The John Howland sailed for the Pacific on October 31, 1839, under Captain William H. Whitfield—the fourth of her fourteen whaling voyages in a career spanning 53 years, from 1830 to 1883. Rerigged as a bark in 1864, the John Howland was wrecked in the Western Arctic, April 17, 1883.

and clean-shaven. He was wearing a jacket [*harure*] and what looked like a close-fitting coat called trousers [*tsuraroji*] or pantaloons [*hatsuerure*] in Oahu. He was nearly six feet tall and looked like a nobleman.

Though Fudenojo and the others didn't know what would become of them after being saved by the foreigners, they were relieved that they were being kept alive, and their means of returning home would present itself in due course.

The following day the captain tried to send Manjiro to the island in a small boat and Manjiro cried bitterly, afraid that he was being sent back to stay. When the captain told him by gestures that he was being sent to help fetch clothing left on the island, he finally understood. Nodding, he and some crewmen returned to the cave and collected their possessions.

"Flag of the United States" and "Flag of the *John James Howland* [sic]"

"Each country has a flag design to identify the ship's origin. They raise this flag at the top of the middle mast when the ship enters a port and stays there." The flag at bottom identifies the ship's owners, John and James Howland. Manjiro evidently confused the name of the ship with the name of the ship's owners. — *Rosenbach Museum & Library*

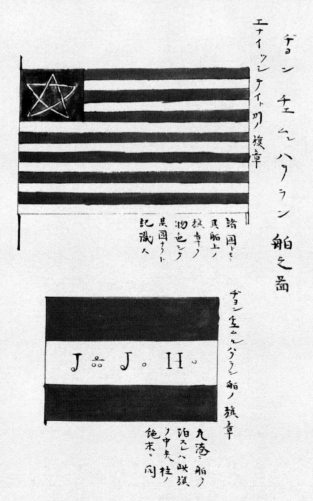

"Drawing of the Ship *John James Howland*"

This painting of the *John Howland* [title appears on previous page with flag illustrations] is made on two separate pages of *Hyoson Kiryaku*. It depicts the ship at anchor but with her sails filled with wind. Perhaps this is the majestic view beheld by the castaways as their rescuers rowed them to safety.

The English caption at the bottom reads: "Captain Wm H Whitfield Fairhaven. She picked up 5 Japanese. They was Hailcain 1851." In addition to the poor grammar in the illustration's caption, the date is incorrect. The rescue took place in 1841. "Hailcain" is phoenetic Japanese for "Hurricane" Island.

As in most of the illustrations taken from copies of *Hyoson Kiryaku*, the English text is likely transcribed by interns or professional transcribers with no knowledge of English. Thus the letters are crude and nearly illegibile.   — *Rosenbach Museum & Library*

CAPT. WM H WHITFIELD : FAIRHAVEN SHECICHBD

RANESE THEI WAS HATLCA IN   18 51

"The Ship's Bow"

Manjiro describes many of his rescuers as being dark-skinned, such as the sailor depicted here looking out over the ship's bow. In the 1840s, many of the New Bedford whalemen were people of color, such as Native Americans, Cape Verdeans, African Americans and West Indians. *— Rosenbach Museum & Library*

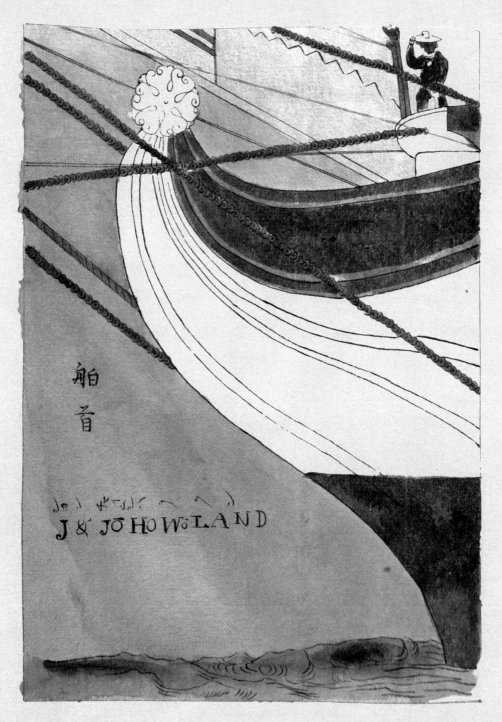

Hull of the *John Howland*

Sailors on deck operate the capstan, which is used to hoist and weigh the anchor, and to haul blubber aboard. *— Rosenbach Museum & Library*

"The Ship's Stern"

"E Pluribus Unum. These letters are said to be used in the United States." — *Rosenbach Museum & Library*

"Meal Bell" and "American People"

In this scene, a young sailor stands in line for his meal as a ship's officer observes. Above his head hangs the ship's bell. The painting pays close attention to the men's style of dress, which was of great interest to the castaways' interrogators. — *Rosenbach Museum & Library*

Soon the ship left the island and headed north in search of whales. In six months, they sailed from the sea off eastern Japan toward the southeast, catching 15 to 16 whales along the way. Fudenojo and the others observed the foreigners' method of catching whales. One man would climb to the top of the mast and look at the distant ocean through a telescope. If he spotted a whale, he signaled the men below and they immediately lowered four small boats. Each boat was manned by a harpooner, a boatheader, and four oarsmen. The boatheader held the helm and the oarsmen pulled on their oars, propelling the boat as fast as if it were flying. When they got close to the whale, the harpooner skillfully threw his harpoon at the vital part on the whale's back. However, whales have different temperaments: Some dive straight to the bottom; some rush through the waves. The crew contemplate the situation then quickly retreat. The whale eventually returns to the place where it had been harpooned. If struck in a vital area, the whale died instantly. If the whale writhed, the men would throw another harpoon into it and stabbed it in the throat with a lance. It died quickly, and they tied it by the flukes and towed it to the ship.

Two Whales

"When I [Shoryo] visited the whaling ground at Kubotsu Village [Kochi] this February and March, I drew two whales and brought back the pictures. I show them here."

"Right whale [top]. This whale is so fat that its length and girth are about the same. The eye is over 17 inches long."

"Humpback whale. Length: 40 feet. These two species are found mostly around Japan and Manjiro said there were more here than in other countries." — *Rosenbach Museum & Library*

"A Picture of a Giant Whale Jumping Around"

"This species of whale is called *sekan* or dry-back whale in our country. They rarely dive to the ocean floor, and often swim with their backs stretched so straight that they sometimes touch it with their tail. Thus, their back seems dry due to the sunshine. Sailors cutting whales say that this is why it was so named. The body seems short as its jumping is observed and sketched from the back side. It sometimes tries to open its mouth. Watching it in the waves, the lower lip is far bigger than the upper one. The eye stretches out and is visible from the back of the whale." – *Rosenbach Museum & Library*

A man jumped down from the ship onto the body, made a hole in the blubber and passed a rope through it. Meanwhile, other crew members working on planks attached to the ship's side, sliced deep cuts through the blubber to the flesh using long spears. The blubber was then pulled from the flesh by winding up the rope by means of a winch. The flesh was left in the sea, ignored. The head was severed and lifted on deck by pulleys. They cut up both the head and the tail, boiling them in a big cauldron on deck to obtain the oil. No firewood was needed in the process, as the dregs of the whale were used for fuel.

"A Picture of Cutting a Whale"

"A whale is cut in four pieces: at the neck [in two], the body, and the tail. Before cutting it, two men descend on it to peel the blubber and make holes for anchors. The head is hung up after cutting it at the neck with a knife. At the last stage, they work on the body by putting ropes through it and roll up the peeled blubber like a scroll. The meat is left as it floats away." — *Rosenbach Museum & Library*

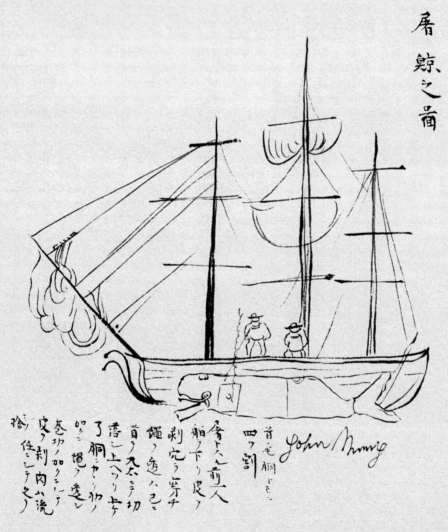

Three Whales

"A sperm whale. Most of the whales caught in the ocean are this kind."

The three whales are labeled in English by John Mung as a "Sperm Whale," "Finback" [center], and "Right Whale." The Japanese characters to the right of the whale at bottom mistakenly identify it as a humpback. *— Rosenbach Museum & Library*

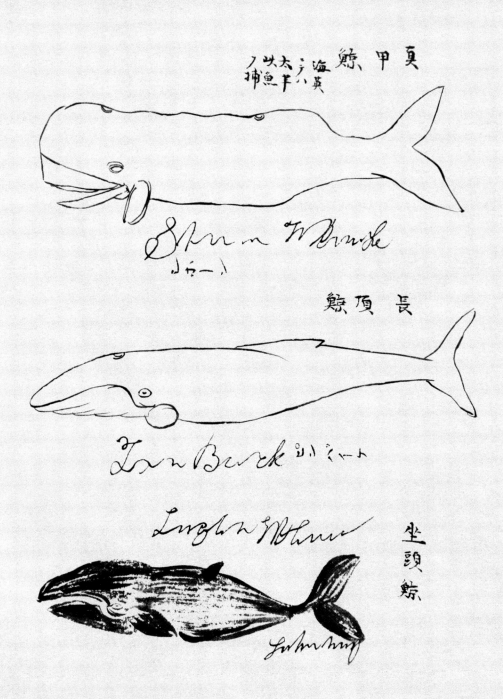

Manjiro's Diagram of the *John Howland*

At right is an overview of the ship showing the bow at top. Manjiro describes the bow: "This part of the ship is bottomless, and after cooking, the waste and slop are washed off through it [the hawsers]." Protruding diagonally from the bow are the cats used to raise the anchors. On the ship's deck, the following objects are labeled [top to bottom]: the foremast, the main mast, and the mizzen mast. Manjiro also drew in hatches, the windlass, the helm, and the wheelhouse.

At left [from top to bottom], Manjiro illustrates and labels: "The base of the mast," where a waterproof seal is visible; the bowsprit, where there is "a hole to tighten straw mats," probably to control the flow of water where the bowsprit joins the bow; and two "small boats" [whale boats] equipped with "harpoons" and oarlocks where "an oar is hung here." — *Rosenbach Museum & Library*

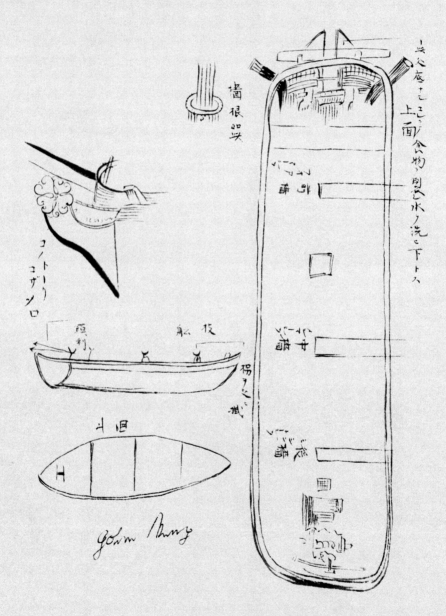

44

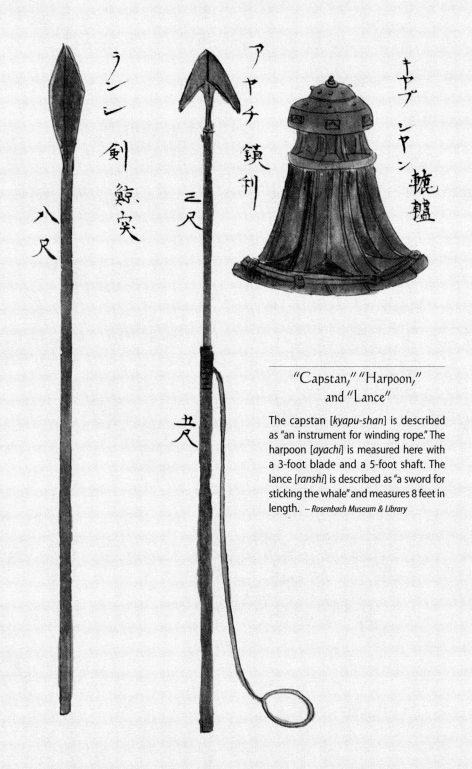

キヤプ シヤン 轆轤

アヤチ 鎮刊

ラ ン シ 剣 鯨 突

八 尺

三 尺

五 尺

"Capstan," "Harpoon," and "Lance"

The capstan [*kyapu-shan*] is described as "an instrument for winding rope." The harpoon [*ayachi*] is measured here with a 3-foot blade and a 5-foot shaft. The lance [*ranshi*] is described as "a sword for sticking the whale" and measures 8 feet in length. *— Rosenbach Museum & Library*

"Pig Tub [tao] for Feeding Pigs"

夕才養豬桶

"Water Pump [bon]"

小ン水湯

ワタアー切水桶

"Water Casket [wadakashika]"

バレロ水桶

"Water Barrel [barero]"

徑四尺尺寸三尺四寸

之三尺已上

堅二丁六分

"Used either for cooling oil or for dispensing drinking water; 4 feet 10 inches in diameter [at center], 3.5 feet in diameter [at top], and 3.5 feet in height." –*Rosenbach Museum & Library*

"Used for storing water or whale oil; 3 inches [stave thickness]."

シトオ 竈

"Stove"

Wood and coal stoves, as well as wood and coal-fired boilers and engines, were of particular interest to the Japanese interrogators. Foreigners at sea were in constant need of provisions such as wood, water, and food, and securing them from Japanese territories was one of the main goals laid down by Commodore Perry in his treaty demands. Manjiro had made a considerable effort to describe the principle of steam-powered engines to his interrogators. The idea of feeding wood or coal into an iron box to generate steam was simple enough, but the ability to create pressure capable of powering such fantastic vehicles as trains and steamships was almost unimaginable. *— Rosenbach Museum & Library*

"Rudder" and "Anchor"

Shoryo's accurate depictions of the anchor and rudder, which includes pintles, are testament to his and Manjiro's knowledge of Western shipbuilding design. *— Rosenbach Museum & Library*

テラ

舵ケ

アンク
錨

Items Aboard Ship

The descriptions identify a candle [*kyanro*], a candlestick holder [*shitayeshi*], a lantern [*rantan*] with glass cover, and two compasses in a binnacle [*bene*], measuring 22.7 inches [1 shaku 9 sun] in height, 14.3 inches [1 shaku 2 sun] in width, and 18.25 inches [1 shaku 5 sun 3 bu] in depth. — *Rosenbach Museum & Library*

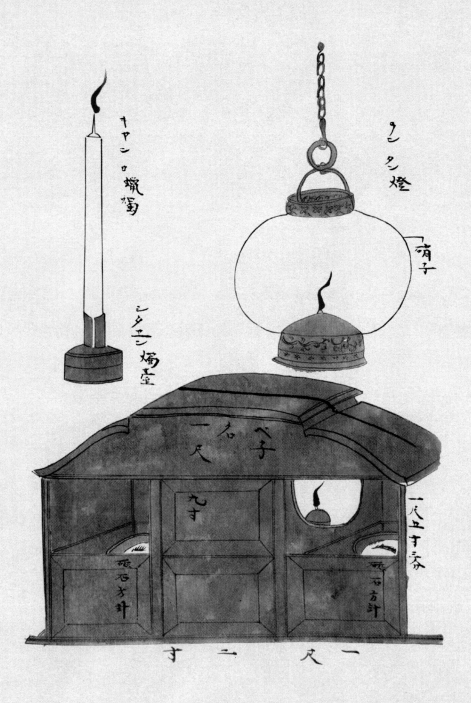

American Tools

Among the multitude of items described by Manjiro to his interrogators are these common objects: a violin and bow, saws, hatchet, hammer, wood plane, grindstone, and gimlet. The toiletry kit [bottom left] includes a looking glass, a comb, and an unidentified item [possibly a razor]. The violin is errantly labeled a banjo in katakana. —*Rosenbach Museum & Library*

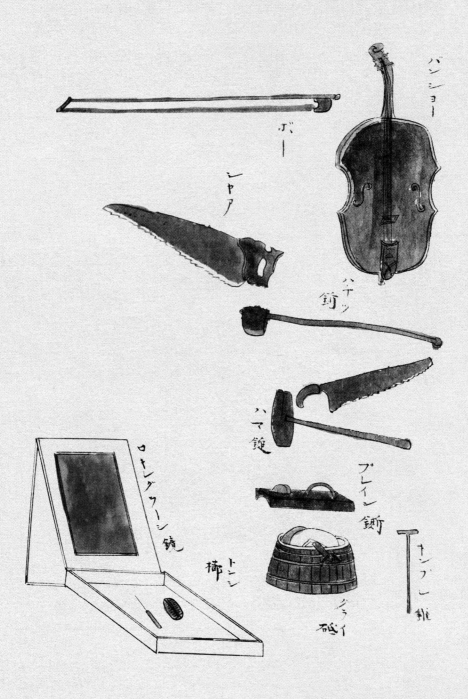

Portrait of a Loved One

"The captain and crew kept pictures of their wives at hand or hung them nearby. They enjoyed seeing them when they went to bed or woke up."

Although this image appears to be a painting of a daguerreotype, it is unlikely that the castaways would have seen such an image on the *John Howland* in 1841. The first daguerreotype artists to practice in New Bedford, O'Brien and Faxon, opened their studio in July of 1841, just three years after its invention in France by Louis Daguerre. By 1849, the year Manjiro left Massachusetts, there were at least five studios operating in downtown New Bedford. Perhaps he was thinking of experiences aboard the *Franklin* and subsequent voyages, or of what he knew to be true. When Manjiro returned to San Francisco in 1860, he purchased a daguerreotype camera. — *Rosenbach Museum & Library*

舶頭等各其妻ノ像シ之ヲ座右ニ懸霞起相ヲ以自娯

Manjiro's Coins

Manjiro's artfully drawn coins include [right to left, top to bottom]: "one dollar gold coin"; the reverse side of a one dollar gold coin; "copper coin" [a penny or half-cent]; "one dollar [*wan dara*] silver coin—weighs 4 monme 8 bu, and is equivalent to 1 kan 500 ketsu Japanese; a half dollar [*has dara*] silver coin—weighs 2 monnme 4 bu, and is equivalent to 750 ketsu Japanese; a quarter dollar—weighs 1 monme 2 bu, and is equivalent to 370 ketsu Japanese; one dime [*wan rayen*]—equivalent to 187.5 ketsu Japanese; a half dime [*has rayen*]—equivalent to 93 ketsu 6 bu Japanese." – *Rosenbach Museum & Library*

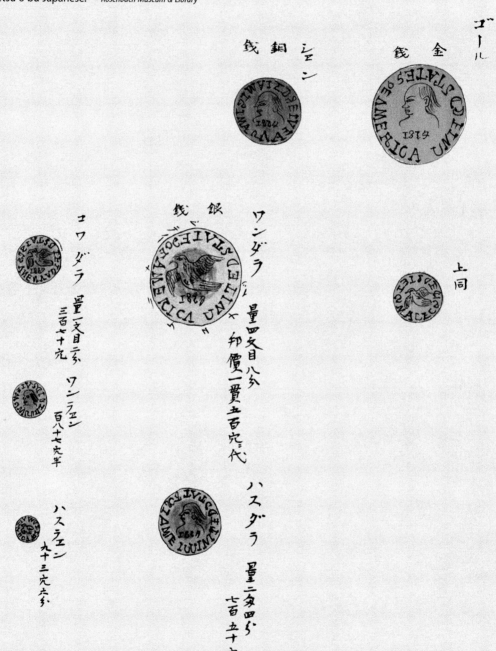

On a day in November, the ship entered port at Oahu, one of the Sandwich Islands. After remaining on the ship for 30 days, Captain Whitfield went ashore, taking the castaways with him to visit his friend Dr. Judd. After they exchanged greetings, the captain told him how he had had the good fortune to rescue these people. Dr. Judd[6] conversed in gestures, asking Fudenojo and the others if they came from a country where people prayed and bowed with their hands pressed together. He showed them 20 pieces of silver, one two-shu gold coin, a copper coin, and a Japanese smoking pipe, and asked if they were from the country that produced these articles. Fudenojo and the rest gestured in the affirmative. Dr. Judd nodded and, by gestures, related this story:

Eight or nine years ago, some people from Osaka were shipwrecked. The captain died and the others were entrusted to an American ship by the good offices of a native man called "Hariryo." They returned to Japan by way of China, and those were the articles they had left behind. At the request of Captain Whitfield, Dr. Judd said the castaways could remain on Oahu and they would be well taken care of. Dr. Judd was originally an American and practiced medicine in Oahu. He had a wife Ohine, a daughter Kinau and five male and female servants.

Later, the castaways were taken to the government office and a local official named Tuhanahawa met them. Next, they went to the inspection office and were asked by gestures about the details of their shipwreck. They were given lodging five houses to the east at the home of Kaukahawa, a subordinate of Tuhanahawa. Kaukahawa's brother, named "Chocho," was gentle and mild by nature and he associated with the men so well that he became attached to them. He went to much trouble for them.

After Fudenojo and the others had settled down, Captain Whitfield had five jackets and five pairs of trousers made for them, and gave them five half-dollars each. The ship's company also gave them five overcoats. The captain told Fudenojo and the others that now that they had settled down, they must live in peace. Then he asked for Fudenojo's permission to take Manjiro to America and educate him. He thought the boy learned quickly and showed great promise. He said he would treat Manjiro well.

Fudenojo was dismayed with the idea that after drifting to such a distant foreign land, they might have to live separately against their wishes. He didn't want them to be separated— they had been through so much adversity together. On the other hand, Captain Whitfield was very kind and had saved their lives; Fudenojo sympathized with him. As the request grew out of the affection and admiration the captain felt for the boy, the decision rested with Manjiro. Fudenojo gave his permission. This pleased Captain Whitfield very much. He took Manjiro with him and returned to the ship.

6. Dr Gerrit Parmele Judd, 1803-73, graduated from medical school in New York in 1825. Two years later, he became a missionary and sailed to Hawaii with his wife. Soon after, he was appointed physician to the American Foreign Missions where he gained the confidence of the king and chiefs. He developed a keen understanding of the Hawaiian character, learned the language, and by 1842, was involved with matters of state. He served under King Kamehameha III as minister of foreign affairs, minister of finance, and de facto prime minister. In 1853 he helped draw up a constitution aimed at preserving the island's independence. Its principle was to create a union of natives with foreigners as subjects. The plan was effective but met resistance from foreigners who eventually forced him out of the government. Judd returned to his medical practice and in later years, devoted himself to the agricultural development of the islands.

Hawaiian Islands

"A map of the 11 Sandwich islands. Oahu Island belongs to this group. Its circumference is more than 170 miles." – *Rosenbach Museum & Library*

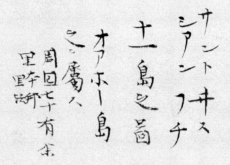

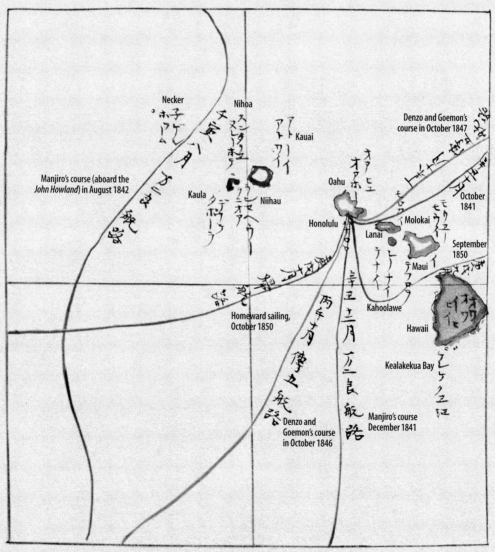

Necker

Nihoa

Kauai

Denzo and Goemon's course in October 1847

Manjiro's course (aboard the *John Howland*) in August 1842

Oahu

October 1841

Kaula

Niihau

Honolulu

Molokai

Lanai

September 1850

Maui

Kahoolawe

Homeward sailing, October 1850

Hawaii

Kealakekua Bay

Denzo and Goemon's course in October 1846

Manjiro's course December 1841

Book Two

Denzo and his brother
had great difficulty in their attempt
to return home to Japan.

After Manjiro left with Captain Whitfield on his whaling ship, Fudenojo and his brother had great difficulty trying to return to Japan. The castaways stayed on Oahu Island through 1841. The island was more than 175 miles around, with 50 coastal villages and a port called Sohahho[1]. Its capital, fronting the harbor, was called Honolulu. Ships from Europe and America cast anchor there, waiting for favorable weather. The port had begun to thrive even more when gold mines were opened in California in 1849. The ships going to and from California never failed to call. People from the West and China had opened new stores in Honolulu where they sold a variety of goods and multicolored fabrics. As it prospered more each year, nearly 2,000 houses were built.

King Kauikeaouli [*Kiyukakeoryo*],[2] ruler of the island, lived in a castle in the capital, a solid building with many large stories. From a distance, one could see that the top story was spacious and could hold hundreds of people. Outside the castle stood the residences of two officials, Tuwanaha and Kanaina, and French priests lived nearby in a large temple, a beautiful structure with a stone tower and glazed windows, a sight of incomparable beauty.

1. *Sohahho* is unidentifiable, though it is probably an English term (possibly South Harbor), as there is no "s" sound in the Hawaiian language.
2. Kauikeaouli is the name King Kamehameha III used before he assumed the throne. He reigned 30 years, 1825-1854.

"A Picture of Ships in the Harbor at Oahu"

— *Rosenbach Museum & Library*

才ア ホ 一島
馬頭之図

"A Picture of Ships in the Harbor at Oahu"

At the time of the castaways' arrival in 1841, Honolulu was a very important port of call for Yankee whalers. It was a friendly island, temperate and bountiful, where ships could repair, refuel, and buy provisions. — *Rosenbach Museum & Library*

The second city, Makai, was located on the southern part of the island with a thousand houses and a fish market on the town's main street. The busy shopping area called "Porenha" was as flourishing as that of the capital. Though this land was close to the equator, the climate was not extremely hot but more like late spring or early summer in Japan. One could not realize a change in temperature unless one was careful to perceive it. Natives who never left the island did not know of frost or snow. Thunder was rare with only an occasional clap in the distance, and the wind was usually from the northeast. If on rare occasions it blew from another quarter, the rains would come suddenly. If the wind shifted round to the northeast again, the rains would let up.

"Oahu Island Flag Design."

"Portrait of the island chief." Manjiro's flag bears the portrait of King Kamehameha III. *– Rosenbach Museum & Library*

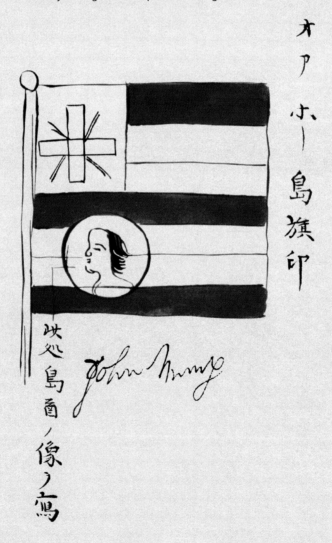

The natives were both intelligent and kind, and honor was an important value. They were tall and yellowish-brown in complexion. Their faces were not powdered but full of natural sleek beauty. Their eyes slanted downward at the corners. Some natives made fun of Goemon, saying Japanese and Chinese people had slanting eyes, and pulled the tails of their eyes upward in mock imitation. Goemon retorted by saying that the foreigners' eyes were like this—and he pulled the tails of his eyes downward. Their hair was jet black, the men's trimmed at the back of the neck and the women's bundled at the crown, and they liked to wear various ornaments. They ate beef and pork and steamed dumplings made from native taro roots, which they put in metal bowls and ate with spoons. When they didn't use spoons, they used their fingertips. They also liked tobacco, which they smoked or chewed, and detested liquor as much as they detested filth. Some people chewed bark to extract the juice and got drunk involuntarily; others were addicted to it. They wore *harore* and pantaloons for clothing.

Their houses were built of stone walls with stone roofs, or of wood with thatched straw roofs and walls and floors painted in deep blue and crimson. The floors were covered with cotton rugs and the people usually sat on chairs. For currency, they used gold, silver and copper coins from the United States. The language was mostly based on American, but they used many vernacular words peculiar to the island. Though Fudenojo and the others had been here for several months, the foreigners could not pronounce his name, perhaps because they had a different tone. So he changed his name to that of his uncle, Denzo.

In Oahu, in May, the thirteenth year of Tempo, the Year of the Tiger [1842], a Japanese man named Zensuke, age 21 or 22, a native of Hyogo, Settsu [Hyogo Prefecture], Japan, came to visit them, accompanied by a cook. He told them this story:

When Zensuke was sailing from Awa [Tokushima Prefecture] to Edo [Tokyo] with a crew of 13 a few years before, they had drifted in a storm and were rescued by a Spanish ship. They were taken to Spain [Mexico],[3] where eleven of the men made a living by cutting down trees and gathering firewood. Zensuke and another crew member stayed with a rich man whose family owned many foreign ships, ran a store, and did business far and wide. Zensuke became acquainted with the national character of the country, spoke the language and learned some letters. He spent his days helping with bookkeeping and doing calculations. One day his benefactor, who had three daughters, advised Zensuke to marry the one he liked best, saying if he remained in Spain, he would not be forsaken for the rest of his life. However, Zensuke was determined to return home to Japan and declined the offer.

Then one day an American merchant ship entered the port en route to China. Zensuke's benefactor begged for passage for five of the 13, as they hoped to return to Japan by way

---

3. Zensuke was captain of the cargo ship, *Eiju-maru*, shipwrecked in October, 1841. After drifting on the Pacific over 100 days and nearly starved, Zensuke and his 12-man crew were rescued by the Spanish pirate ship, *Ensayo*. Forty days later, the castaways were forced to leave the ship at Cape San Lucas in Baja California, Mexico. Zensuke and another castaway, Hatsutaro (described here as a cook) got passage on the American brig *Abigail Adams*, under Captain Doane, enroute to Macao via Honolulu, in 1842. They returned to Nagasaki on a Chinese ship in December, 1843.

of China. Permission was granted. On her way, the ship stopped in Honolulu where, they had heard, several Japanese were living. Zensuke and another left the ship; the other three remained on board. Though the captain accepted 100 silver half dollars a head for passage and promised solemnly to treat them as guests, he went back on his promise, was rude and threatened to flog them to make them work harder.

At this point, Zensuke begged Denzo [formerly Fudenojo] and his companions to get passage on the ship for the return to Japan. They would all have better luck if the number of Japanese increased by even one person. Denzo thought if he took this chance to return to Japan, his life would be so much better. Acting on Zensuke's advice, he applied to a government office for passage. Though the official immediately relayed the request to the ship, the captain would not give permission. Zensuke was sorry he could not have his way, but he wished them well. He added that the other eight were still in Spain and asked Denzo to take pity on them if they ever called at this port. Denzo, Goemon and Zensuke expressed mutual regret at parting. (Zensuke had elegant features and was indescribably kind and gentle by nature. Probably for that reason he was patronized in Spain [Mexico]. He showed a marvelous gold ornament called a *kura*,[4] which was worn by Spanish noblemen on their shoulders. He had received this as a parting gift.)

Having nothing to do after they parted from Zensuke, the castaways sought amusements and sometimes took out small fishing boats with seven or eight natives. They stayed several miles offshore fishing for bonito with a long rod like those used in Japan's seas. If they had a large catch, they took it to market. People in Oahu marveled that Denzo and the others caught such a large amount of fish with a strange rod.

An acquaintance, Kaukahawa, and several of his relatives had a fief in a village more than three miles out of town and engaged in farming. The castaways worked on the farm and collected a rice allowance for their labor. One day Denzo and the others paid them a visit and, as a token of their gratitude for supporting them, helped to draw water and did some cooking. They ended up living there for more than a year. At this time, the men had a rough understanding of the vernacular and wanted to earn a living serving someone. When they spoke to their guardian, the person responsible for them, he told them not to worry, to spend the days as before and their upkeep would be taken care of. But the castaways were not happy and petitioned an official with their wish to serve someone. They were granted permission to do so.

Doctor Judd, who had practiced medicine, was now a government official and had changed his name to Opunikauka. Because he worried about the castaways, they went to him to find people they could serve. Dr. Judd agreed, and the men were distributed among his relatives and acquaintances. Denzo served Miss [Mishi] Kuuke, a teacher from America. (All respectable people were addressed as Miss or Mr. [Meshite], the honorific titles of the land.) Jusuke and Goemon served Dr. Judd, though Goemon was still too young to be assigned

---

4. *Kura* is a translation of the Spanish word *charretera*, meaning epaulets. As a parting gift, Zensuke's benefactor, Comandante Francisco, gave him a pair of epaulets to wear on his uniform.

a task and was told to look after the children. Toraemon was employed by a carpenter and eventually learned the craft.

In foreign countries, church services are generally held on every seventh day, called Sunday [*Shonrei*]. This festival was observed even during a voyage. People assembled from ten in the morning till noon. The head priest set up an altar and offered dumplings, called taasu, made by kneading barley flour with oil. Then he preached a sermon. The services were quite different from the Buddhist service. They began with a reading of the national laws and regulations, then the priest preached the principle of the five cardinal virtues. This service usually took place four times a month, much like our five seasonal festivals. On this day, people took a holiday and amused themselves. In the villages, people bolted their front doors and went on outings. The day after Sunday was called *Poakahi*; the second day, *Poalua* [*Hoarutsu*]; the third day, *Poakolu* [*Poakoru*]; the fourth, *Poaha*; the fifth, *Poalima* [*Hoaarima*]; the sixth, *Poaono* [*Hoamororo*]; and back to *Shonrei* again.[5] This rotation was repeated four times to make a month. Wages were paid every fourth Sunday.

During Sunday services the following September or October, Denzo learned that an American ship with two Japanese aboard had anchored at Sohahho in Honolulu harbor. (Children of the island came and went in small boats to the anchored ships to trade in foods. Consequently, such news was imparted by them.) When Denzo saw some people landing at the harbor entrance, he decided to inquire where the ship was from. Running as fast as his legs could take him, he raced toward the wharf. There, he saw a man getting on a small boat from the big ship. As his features suggested that he was Japanese, Denzo addressed him. Smiling, the man ran up to him and answered yes, that his name was Yasutaro and he came from Edo.

Yasutaro was about twenty years old and had been on his way home to Edo from Mutsu [Aomori Prefecture] with a crew of eight in a ship carrying salt when the ship began to drift. They remained at sea for about a year and ran out of provisions. Racking their brains for means of obtaining food, they miraculously came upon a school of tuna and were able to catch some. They dried and ate them, but their good fortune didn't last. Six of the men eventually died from hunger and thirst. Only he and Tobei survived. They were saved by an American whaling ship.

They deserted their ship with the dead lying in it, transferred to the whaling ship, and now reached this land. Saying it must be providence to meet Denzo, he bought some beef and quickly headed back to his ship to tell Tobei the news. After a while Yasutaro brought Tobei, who was about thirty years old, ashore to meet Denzo. They greeted each other and trekked to Denzo's lodgings. Tobei explained to Denzo that the captain's wife and three children were on board and the Japanese survivors were told to look after the children. Because of the captain's family, it would be too inconvenient for the big ship to return them to Japan. However, a French ship was in port waiting to sail for China, so the captain asked for their passage on that ship and they hoped to go aboard shortly.

---

5. With the exception of *Shonrei* [Sunday], all of the weekdays are given in the Hawaiian language.

Since Denzo and the others could understand some foreign languages, including French, they had to go and ask personally if they could board the French ship too. They went together and, with Tobei's help in communicating, Denzo made the request. But the captain refused, saying he had consented to take two men aboard and it would be difficult to take more. Distraught, Denzo jumped to his feet and proposed that if they were to pay their fare in advance, the captain would surely consent. However, because they had made no preparations and didn't have enough money, he was obliged to give up.

Then Tobei and the others intervened with the idea to raise money by selling the Japanese clothes that belonged to the six men who had starved to death. However, nobody would buy them, as Japanese clothes were not worn in foreign countries. Going on board, they pressed their request but the captain refused to consent. (Denzo and his companions went aboard ship several times and occasionally had a meal, which made the cooks angry. The visitors pretended not to notice.) Finally they parted in tears, hoping to meet each other again someday. Soon afterwards, Tobei and Yasutaro transferred to the French ship and left port.

In the first year of Koka, the Year of the Snake [1844], Jusuke became lame from his injured leg, which had never healed. Perhaps that caused him a complication, which became incurable after a short time. Opunikauka [Dr. Judd] gave them money for treatment and was attentive in every way. One day he told Denzo and Goemon he wished to secure treatment for Jusuke and save his life at any cost, but because he was no longer a practicing physician he could not obtain the proper medicine. He said a good doctor lived in a village called Koolau, about seven miles away. They would have to take Jusuke there immediately and get help.

To carry Jusuke they bought a palanquin, then bid farewell to Opunikauka and hurried on. They had not gone three miles when they saw someone leading a horse in the opposite direction. The man bowed to Denzo and his companions and said he was from the village. He had come to meet them at Opunikauka's request. The men were surprised and delighted at that unexpected news. As Jusuke lay comfortably in the palanquin, Denzo asked the man on horseback to carry Jusuke so he could ride the horse.

Denzo arrived at Koolau ahead of the others and sought lodging at the house of a man called Puupun, where four people lived in the household including Puupun's brother, Tetsuhani, and his wife. Denzo visited the doctor on the same day, giving him Opunikauka's message, but the doctor was already informed. Jusuke was taken to him at once and received treatment. As it happened, the head priest of the American church located in the village—a man named *Parikeya* [Parker][6]—had been a neighbor of Captain William H. Whitfield. This connection influenced the doctor to administer various sorts of medicine and pay attention to the castaways in all matters.

---

6. Rev. Benjamin W. Parker, 1803-77, and his wife Mary Elizabeth Barker Parker, 1805-1907, arrived at the Sandwich Islands from Connecticut in May 1833. The Parkers established a successful mission in Kaneohe, Oahu, where they remained at least until the early 1850s. Benjamin Parker became principal of the Native Hawaiian Theological School. Both he and his wife died in Honolulu. An elementary school in Kaneohe is named in his honor.

"Banana Fruit"

"Banana [*munana*] or Japanese *basho*. Its flower is called *maiya*, the same as in our country. The picture is the actual size. They are reddish-yellow and resemble the color of a ripe orange. They taste extremely sweet. People who are in a hurry to bring them to trade, ripen them in steam. Because Oahu has a uniform climate, fruits like this are available year round." – *Rosenbach Museum & Library*

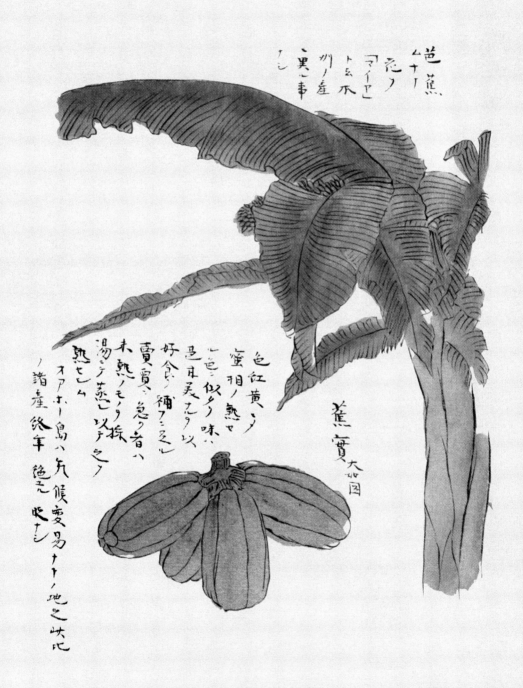

In the second year of Koka, the Year of the Horse [1845], neither good medicine nor good care proved effective for Jusuke, who died at age 31 in Koolau,[7] Oahu, in early January. Denzo and Goemon deeply mourned his death, as they had relied on him immensely. They laid his body in a coffin in accordance with the regulation of the land and buried it outside the temple in the nearby village of Kaneohe. Mr. Parker recited something similar to a Buddhist text and was especially cordial as he addressed the last words to the departed soul. From that time on, Goemon lodged at the temple of Parker while Denzo continued to live at the house of Puupun.

It was customary for Kekauluohi [*Kinikakeoryoha*],[8] the ruler, to make an annual tour of the island, and she visited the village accompanied by the head official, Tutunahawa. When the official stayed at the house of Puupun, he saw Denzo and asked about his health and how he was getting along. Grateful for Tutunahawa's kindness, Denzo said he had been too depressed to work since Jusuke had died in the spring. However, he had had a chance to look around the area and it seemed to him there was much wasted land there. He asked permission of the magistrate to arrange for them to reclaim it.

Tutunahawa complied and at their request he called some natives to help Denzo with the work and gave directions before he left. With everybody's help, they built a hut on a beach about five miles from Jusuke's grave. They cleared some fields and grew taros, sweet potatoes, corn, millet, and gourds and engaged in farming every day. As this land was recently opened for settlement, they were glad to have so many people clear fields. Because no land tax had to be paid, people were free to cultivate more extensively. (Men over 15 had to pay a half dollar and women paid one quarter for a poll tax. However, Denzo and the others were never ordered to pay, perhaps because they were not counted.)

In late September Captain Whitfield again visited the island. As soon as he learned that the castaways lived in Koolau, he visited the village and found Goemon at Sunday service at the American chapel. The two men excitedly congratulated each other for being safe and healthy. Then Goemon explained that Jusuke had died and Fudenojo had changed his name to Denzo. Goemon went to fetch Denzo and the captain was delighted to see him.

The captain mourned Jusuke's death and told them that Manjiro was well. He knew they lived on the beach and said their house must have a fine view and that when he left the church with Parker, he intended to visit. Denzo and Goemon hurried home ahead of them so they could clean up the house and set up pickle tubs as temporary chairs. Soon the captain and Parker arrived. Sitting down, Captain Whitfield envied them their house and said jokingly that its structure did not become the surroundings. Producing two silver coins, he gave them to the brothers. Before he left, he told Goemon to find time to visit Sohahho within a few days because he had something else to give him.

---

7. Jusuke was laid to rest in a small cemetery in Kaneohe, Oahu. Today, just beyond his gravestone near the Kamehameha Highway stands the Benjamin Parker Elementary School.

8. Kekauluohi was the former wife of Kamehameha II and the premier under the reigning king, Kamehameha III.

The next day Goemon visited Captain Whitfield's ship and thanked him for his kindness. Because they had drifted thousands of miles away from Japan and were unhappy, the captain said he had intended to send them home as soon as possible but had not been able to make good on his intention. But now there was a ship bound for the sea off Japan and he wanted to request permission for them to go aboard. If they truly wished to return home, they must get ready quickly, come to his ship and stay aboard. He gave them five jackets, five trousers, shoes, two rolls of white cloth and some tobacco. Goemon heartily thanked Captain Whitfield and

---

"A Gourd" and "A Pumpkin [ipufuu]"

"Gourds are used for receptacles containing clothing and food. They are also substituted for pails containing water. They are used for numerous purposes.

"Denzo had gathered various fruits different from domestic ones and put them in cans. Though he brought them to Japan, he could not find them when he looked for them after landing in Loochoo. Probably somebody on board had stolen them. Length: 2 feet or so." – *Rosenbach Museum & Library*

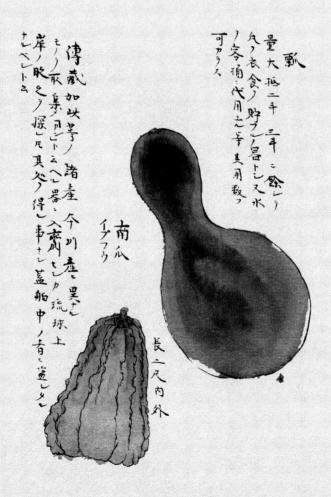

hurried back to tell Denzo the news. Both men were moved to tears by the captain's kindness. Then they gave their cultivated land to the former owner and their old friends. They left their house and said good-bye to everyone.

Then they called on the head priest and bade him farewell, thanking him for his kindness. Parker gave them jackets and two handkerchiefs, which Denzo and Goemon respectfully accepted. They left Koolau in early October with four ducks, six chickens, two gamecocks, two pigs, and two hoes. First they went to Honolulu to bid farewell to Dr. Judd and others. Then they went on board Captain Whitfield's ship and shared what they had brought. However, Captain Whitfield never mentioned Toraemon. When Denzo spoke to him and asked whether he had told Toraemon about this plan, he shook his head, saying Toraemon had been unfriendly to him and he did not intend to worry about him.

Amazed, Denzo said that Toraemon had been a neighbor of his and had been employed by him on the fishing boat that had drifted out to sea. If they deserted him they would not know what to say to his family back home. On his knees Denzo begged Captain Whitfield to secure passage for him too. The captain replied that he had secured passage for only two people and it would be difficult to add more. However, he heard that another big ship was due to sail for the sea off Japan and he would try to make arrangements for their friend. He succeeded in getting Toraemon passage on that ship and asked him to get ready quickly. Toraemon met with Captain Whitfield, thanked him, bade a sad farewell to the brothers, and they went aboard their respective ships.

Both were American whaling ships. Denzo and Goemon embarked on the ship named *Florida* with Captain Arthur Cox.[9] When their ship was about to set sail, Toraemon appeared at the bow of the other ship and beckoned the brothers, saying loudly that he was planning to disembark and wished them a safe voyage. Hearing this, Denzo hurried to Toraemon's ship and asked what the trouble was. Toraemon said that the captain was unkind and he felt uncomfortable. Denzo tried to reason with him in many ways, but Toraemon refused to reconsider. While Denzo persisted the ship weighed anchor, so Denzo departed and returned to his ship. It was later learned that the ship from which Toraemon disembarked visited Japan on that voyage and had her rigging repaired at Uraga.

Leaving Oahu far behind, Denzo's ship sailed southwest for several days, stopping at a bald, barren island [Hadaka Jima] on its way from New Guinea to Australia. The island consisted of sand and a small hill with groves of coconut palms. These trees looked like hemp palms without branches and the leaves grew from the base like bundled cattails. The

---

9. Whaleships commonly discharged individual crewmen in Hawaiian ports and replaced them with temporary men, who signed on for comparatively short, seasonal whaling cruises. (Herman Melville made at least two such cruises in the Pacific in the 1840s). These were mostly footloose sailors "on the beach," as well as native Hawaiians and, now, Manjiro's two Japanese companions. Such temporary hands were usually brought back to Hawaii at the end of the cruise. The 523-ton ship *Florida* was built at New York City in 1821 and made only one whaling voyage out of New Bedford, sailing on August 4, 1845, bound for the Indian Ocean and Northwest Coast grounds under Captain Arthur Cox. She returned to New Bedford on May 2, 1850, with an unusually large catch. The *Florida* next carried passengers to the California Gold Rush (1849–50), then returned to whaling, completing three voyages from Fairhaven (1851–61) and two from San Francisco (1868–70) before she was wrecked in the Arctic in 1871 on her seventh whaling voyage.

"A Picture of Naked Natives, Males and Females"

Other than "a palm tree," no information is given for this painting of the friendly natives of Hadaka Jima. On the horizon, the ship at anchor could be the *Florida*. — *Rosenbach Museum & Library*

largest fruit resembled gourds and hung among the leaves. Covered with a rough rind, they looked like human faces with three dents or two eyes and a mouth. Inside was a hard crust and deeper inside was meat and juice. The meat was like walnut and the juice like milk. One felt cool and refreshed eating the meat, which tasted incomparably good. However, each fruit usually contained a pint of juice and it was impossible to drink it all at a gulp.

The men of the island wore no clothes, but the women sewed some palm leaves together which only covered their lower front. The men's hair was trimmed at the back and their mustaches and beards were completely plucked out. It was impossible to tell men from women except by their private parts.

"A Picture of Naked Natives Living in a Hole"

— Rosenbach Museum & Library

裸夷穴居之圖

For shelter they dug a hole in the ground, placed palm trees over the opening, roofed it with palm leaves and made a burrow. They had no cooking utensils. For food they roasted seaweed on spits and drank palm juice, which made them stink of palm oil. Women repeatedly applied palm oil to their faces and bodies as they valued the smell and it made their skin glossy.

As the *Florida* gradually neared the beach, islanders, men and women, rowed over to the ship in small boats carved out of palm trees and tied with woven palm fronds. They competed with each other in scrambling up the ship's side to go aboard. The ship's crew took naked women to the bunks in return for tobacco and rings. Some shameless, vigorous men had sexual intercourse openly. Naked men stood by and watched, smoking. Penises were erect and glandes were jumping. Though some pointed to others and laughed, the crew paid no attention. After the young men had finished their dalliance, the naked women, who seemed to have a little sense of shame, put their legs together and covered their private parts with their hands. But if they were asked to show them, they spread their legs a little and struck other obscene postures. It was customary for natives of the island to act this way in return for items like tobacco and food.

One day Denzo met a man on the island who was grimy, in rags, and looked different from the natives. When he observed him closely he was surprised to recognize someone he had known in Oahu. Asked what had brought him there, the man replied that he had been transported because he had committed a crime. However, he felt that the crude manner of the islanders was no different from beasts. They didn't even have a conception of farming. He had found some flat land at the foot of the mountains and grew sweet potatoes and corn there. He also carved out a palm tree and made a fertilizer pail out of it, collecting natives' excrement for use as manure. He told his story so pitifully that Denzo took off his clothes and gave them to him.

Not only coconut palm trees but other trees called breadfruit [*buressuru*] grew on the islands in this region. Their fruit is similar to a sweet potato and edible.

In January, the third year of Koka, the Year of the Sheep [1846], their ship sailed north and entered port at Gyuan [Guam] in the Ladrone [Mariana] Islands. On the same day the captain landed, he found lodging at a ship brokerage while the crew took turns lodging at inns. This was a good port and houses stood close together amid lovely hills and high mountains in the background. In the marketplace were products from both mountains and the sea. Few neighboring islands could match this one in prosperity. They had sufficient wood and water and they grew rice and cultivated crops year round in a climate that was not too hot. The language and dress style of the natives closely resembled those of Oahu and Spain.[10] Here they repaired their ship.

About late January they set sail and headed north. In the middle of March, they reached Japanese waters and neared Hachijo Island.[11] Denzo and Goemon were much encouraged to

10. "Spain" actually refers to the Spanish territories of California, Texas and Mexico..
11. Hachijo Island is a volcanic Island which belongs to the Izu Islands group. It is located 180 miles south of Tokyo.

"A Map of Gyuan [Guam] Island"

"Its circumference is more than 120 miles." Guam, in the Mariana Islands, was a popular stop for American ships. A beautiful island with numerous hills and a large mountain, it provided mariners with fresh water and wood fuel. Rice and other grains were plentiful year round. Ships underwent minor repairs in Guam, and letters to and from home were exchanged between crews.

Manjiro made several visits here on both the *John Howland* and the *Franklin*. Denzo and Goemon also stopped here on their unsuccessful attempt to return home. While in Guam, Manjiro took the time to write a letter to his dear friend and benefactor, Captain Whitfield. The letter was carried by another American ship returning home. The text of the letter appears in the Appendix. — *Rosenbach Museum & Library*

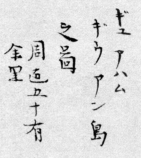

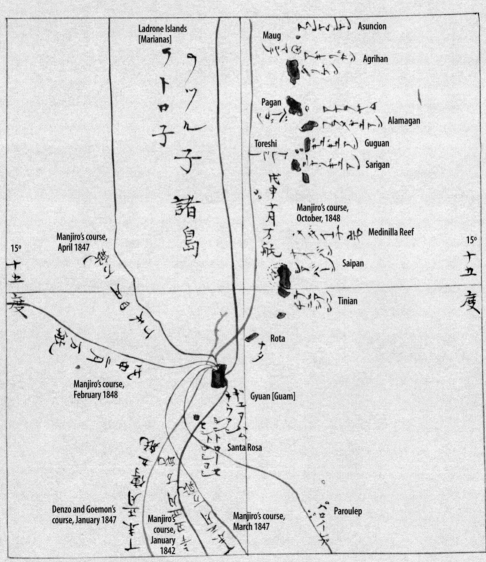

be so near. The captain expected to see Japanese people and their houses for the first time. The captain and some crew rowed toward shore, carrying a letter which said Denzo and Goemon had been under his care and would be returning to Japan. They got near enough to see houses and human figures cultivating fields with drawn horses and oxen. However, the wind was strong and the waves rose and they could not bring their boat near a beach. They kept sailing around the island from dawn to nightfall, trying to approach it, but to no avail.

They left Hachijo Island and headed north-northeast to Ezo [Hokkaido], rounded the edge of a mountain and headed straight north. When they finally approached the shore, still in Japanese waters, they could see smoke and fires along the coastline. The situation was confusing to the crew, but Denzo had learned that coastal defenses had been established to warn against approaching foreign ships. Unconcerned, Denzo lowered the small boat and went ashore with his brother and an officer. When Denzo looked about for the people he had seen by the smoking fires, they had disappeared. Not a soul could be seen. He called out, saying he was Japanese, but received no response at all.

Discovering a hut nearby, they visited it, only to find it vacant. But the oven was still hot and various tools were lying around, suggesting that the people had fled recently. Denzo begged the officer to leave them there in Japan's northern country. No doubt the natives had hidden because they were frightened by the big ship. When the ship left the shore, the natives would reappear. The officer shook his head and said that unless he handed them over to the natives with the documents and received a receipt from Japan, he would be at a loss about what to tell Captain Whitfield. Disheartened, Denzo and Goemon returned to the ship and the ship left Ezo.

Though it was now April, it was severely cold. As they headed north, they found numerous sea otters floating on the sea and caught several hundred whales. After sailing about 50 days they reached the foot of the mountains of the Aleutian Islands [*Rushin*] off Russia [*Roshia*]. Snow had accumulated year after year on the high mountain peaks and they shone faintly luminous in the distance, going on for many miles.

As they penetrated the recesses of the northern sea, a boundless expanse of fog hovered over them as far as the eye could see. With no sunshine, day and night were indistinguishable. When a ship happened to pass by, both vessels signaled by striking a piece of wood or beating the gunwale. The clear waves had turned into earth-colored, turbid currents that ran in many directions and snow fell in the bitter cold. Unable to find any whales, they shifted the helm and left the Aleutian area. Passing several small, nearly barren islands in the area, they finally caught several whales.

On a day in September, they sailed with a west wind into a storm. The ship was being tossed so violently in the teeth of the wind, they unfurled the lowest sails, but the ship, large as it was, flew ahead, swayed by the big waves. They could not cook meals for three whole days and ate nothing but steamed vegetable [*bechiteeburu*] dumplings. After about thirty days, the wind shifted to the east and they headed southwest. Six days later they were back on Oahu Island.

Korean Peninsula and Southern Japan

The map below and on the opposite page can be joined to form a composite of Japan and the Korean Peninsula. The routes of Denzo and Goemon aboard the *Florida* in 1845-46, and of Manjiro's whaling voyage in 1846-49 aboard the *Franklin*, show how close the castaways came to touching their homeland—even skirting the volcanic island that once held their lives so tenuously. — *Rosenbach Museum & Library*

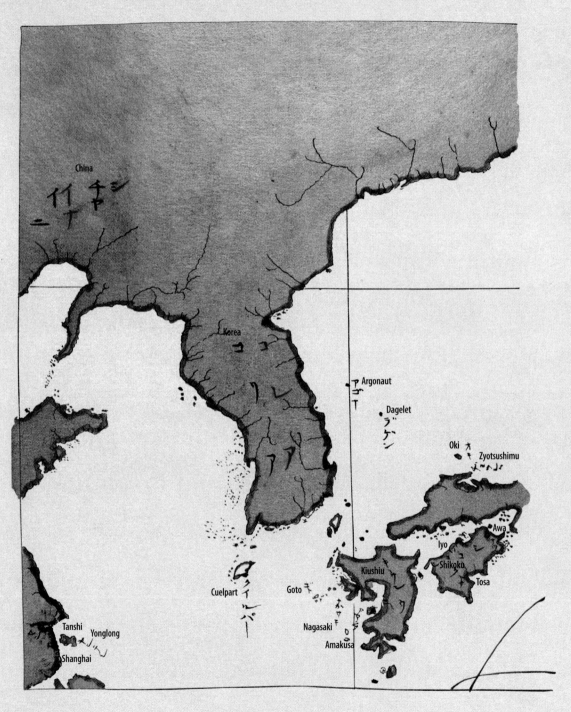

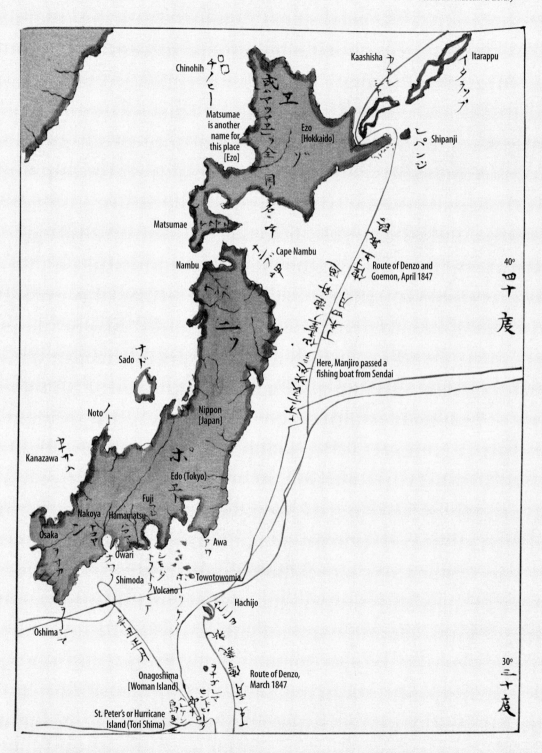

Chinohih

Kaashisha

Itarappu

Matsumae is another name for this place [Ezo]

Ezo [Hokkaido]

Shipanji

Matsumae

Cape Nambu

40°

Nambu

Route of Denzo and Goemon, April 1847

Sado

Here, Manjiro passed a fishing boat from Sendai

Noto

Nippon [Japan]

Kanazawa

Edo (Tokyo)

Fuji

Nakoya

Hamamatsu

Osaka

Owari

Awa

Shimoda

Towotowomia

Volcano

Hachijo

Oshima

30°

Onagoshima [Woman Island]

Route of Denzo, March 1847

St. Peter's or Hurricane Island (Tori Shima)

Book Three

While Denzo and the others struggled futilely to
return to Japan, Manjiro experienced life at sea on
Captain Whitfield's whaling ship before beginning
a new chapter in America.

*I*n November, the twelfth year of Tempo, the Year of the Ox [1841], Manjiro parted from Fudenojo (now Denzo) and the others and accompanied Captain Whitfield on his travels at sea. He was called John Mung, or "Mung" for short, and he became part of the crew.

In early December, they set sail from Oahu and headed south. After sailing for about 30 days, they reached Drummond Island in the Kingsmill Islands [Kiribati], a group of about 30 islands. Some were as close to each other as 2.5 miles, others were 30 miles apart. Drummond's perimeter was over 50 miles around, and it was located right on the equator.

Since the climate was torrid, the natives were nearly naked, wearing only woven palm leaves that hung like a straw raincoat around the waist, barely hiding their private parts. Their hair was cut at the shoulders, and some bundled theirs at the crown. They adorned them-

---

"A Map of Kingsmill Island Group in the Gilbert Islands [Kiribati]"

Presently known as Kiribati, and located 2,800 miles northeast of Australia, this group of 16 coral atolls are covered with coconut palm and pandanus. — *Rosenbach Museum & Library*

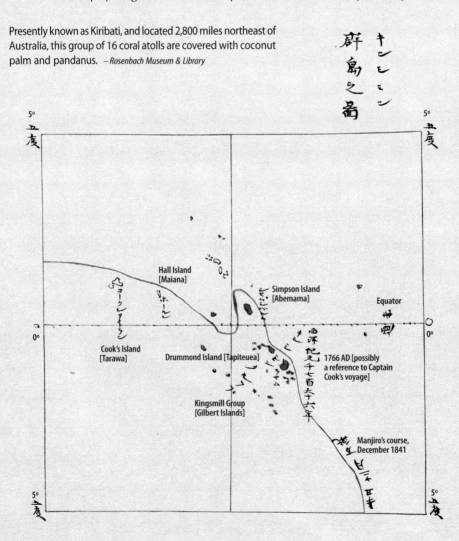

selves in various ways according to their taste. The island was sandy and no grain grew there. The people collected palm nuts and caught fish and lobsters in the area which made up their diet. Their houses were generally crude as they put up four palm posts, roofed them over with palm leaves and covered the floor with palm leaves.

The ship headed due west and sailed for many weeks. In March, the thirteenth year of Tempo, the Year of the Tiger [1842], they arrived in Guam. Here they obtained wood, water and taro. In late April, they weighed anchor and headed northwest, passing through the Sea of Formosa and turning toward Japanese waters. They came upon the volcanic isle called Hurricane Island where the castaways had experienced such hardships together. The men fished for small fish near the island and then caught some whales in waters about 120 to 250 miles off Japan. Sailing east in August, they neared Oahu again, but the wind and waves were

"A Map of Eimeo [Moorea] Islands"

"Its circumference is a little more than 7.3 miles." – *Rosenbach Museum & Library*

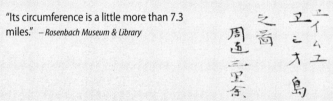

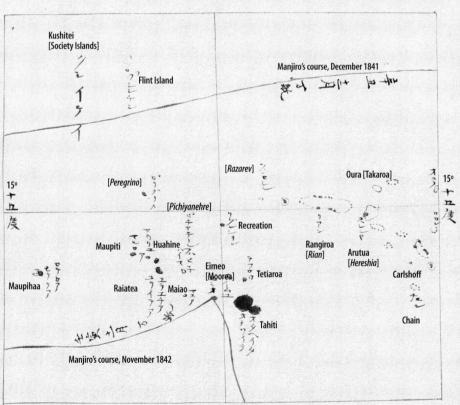

violent and they could not get to the entrance of the harbor. Instead, they turned southwest and in November they reached Eimeo Island, with a perimeter of about 70 miles and a fine harbor. Over 300 houses stood side by side and the people and customs closely resembled those of Oahu. Here they bought wood and water for their journey, and in December they set sail toward the southeast.

By late April in the fourteenth year of Tempo, the Year of the Hare [1843], they had sailed to within 250 miles of Cape Horn, the southern tip of South America. The sea turned icy and numerous large icebergs towered high around them. They passed the highest and largest one, which measured over 1,000 feet and appeared about to topple over. Many passing ships were torn and wrecked on the icebergs. A strange ocean animal the size of a large bull was found

---

"A Picture of a Seal"

"In all severely cold regions, beasts of this species swim about in groups. Cape Horn, above all, abounds in nameless birds and animals." *— Rosenbach Museum & Library*

here and was known as a sea horse [walrus]. Many of them passed the edge of the icebergs with their young. Seals passed by here too, odd and colorful with dark red backs and horns at the tips of their muzzles, all heading northeast. The men also saw a strange star called a comet[1] that filled the western sky. It was said to appear every 80 or 100 years.

The ship headed due north-northwest and it reached the entrance of New Bedford [*Nu Behho*] harbor in early June. New Bedford was located in the province of Massachusetts, in the United States, in North America. The city's harbor was more than six miles long, and the entrance at its narrowest was over two miles wide. An islet in the center of the harbor was

1. This was probably the Great March Comet of 1843, which appeared in the western sky between February and April.

"A Picture of a Horse"

It's possible that this animal is supposed to be a walrus [sea horse] or elephant seal. Perhaps the animal Manjiro described was beyond Shoryo's imagination. — *Rosenbach Museum & Library*

connected with a wooden bridge to the land on the right and left side. The middle board of the bridge to the right was 50 feet long and connected to the adjoining boards with chain rope. The edge of either side was fitted with a wheel. When a ship approached the bridge with its masts standing, a crewman got on the bridge and wound the chain rope with the wheel. The middle board was moved to one side until the ship had passed through. When the rope was unwound, the middle board moved back into place and the bridge reverted to its original state. Passing through the open bridge, they reached berth in New Bedford, mooring their ship in front of the ship owner's house, and set a watch.[2]

After informing the owner of the ship's return, Captain Whitfield parted from the crew. Taking Manjiro with him, he crossed the bridge to the south side[3] and arrived in the village of Fairhaven [*Hahebun*], which was second to New Bedford in number of streets, thoroughfares

2 The *John Howland* returned to New Bedford on May 7, 1843, after a three-and-a-half year whaling voyage with a handsome cargo that included 2,761 barrels of sperm oil.

3. Fairhaven is east of New Bedford.

"A Picture of the Draw Bridge at New Bedford"

Built in 1832, Manjiro's draw bridge was a relatively new design and required a toll to cross. After making berth on the New Bedford side, Captain Whitfield could have crossed over to Fairhaven by ferry or by hiring a horse-drawn cab. A newly-formed company's chic two-wheeled safety cabs provided service from any part of New Bedford to Fairhaven for five cents. – *Rosenbach Museum & Library*

又ーバンフホーー引き橋之圖

80

and houses. Captain Whitfield's house was located in the middle of town. When he reached home the front door was tightly shut and the house looked desolate and dilapidated. Very worried, he knocked at the house next door and asked why his house looked abandoned. Captain Whitfield learned that his wife had died while he was at sea[4] and that because there were no other family members to occupy it, the house was closed up. Devastated, he took Manjiro to the home of James Allen,[5] a carpenter, who gave Manjiro lodging.

4. Manjiro apparently misunderstood the situation. Captain Whitfield's wife died in 1837, two years before his voyage. He became engaged to marry Albertina Peters Keith of Bridgewater prior to leaving port in 1839.
5. There was no James Allen. Whitfield initially put Manjiro under the care of his friend and neighbor, Eben Aiken. Later, he visited another neighbor, Jane Allen, a public school teacher, to arrange a tutorship for Manjiro.

"A Picture of the Waterfront of New Bedford"

This view of the New Bedford waterfront reflects a decidedly oriental perspective. It is difficult to imagine that Manjiro would instruct the artist to include mountains or pagoda-like structures.. — *Rosenbach Museum & Library*

ヌーバッホー 港頭之圖

The country of the United States was more than 2,840 miles [6,930 ri] from east to west, and more than 1,680 miles [4,100 ri] from north to south. It was divided into more than 30 provinces such as Massachusetts, Maine, New York, Pennsylvania, New Hampshire, Rhode Island, Kentucky, Connecticut, Ohio, Indiana, Maryland, North Carolina, South Carolina, Delaware, Mississippi, Illinois, Louisiana, Michigan, Columbia, New Jersey, Alabama, Missouri, Virginia, Georgia, Florida, Tennesse, and so on.

Because the country was located at 40 to 50 degrees north latitude, the air was clean and the temperature was seasonable and a variety of grains grew there. The natives were extremely lovely in appearance, with fair skin and dark hair. They were more than five or six feet tall. Kind and gentle by nature, both affectionate and compassionate, they thought highly of morality and fidelity and were always diligent and industrious in everything, including trading far and wide. Needless to say, the women were lovely and bundled their dark hair at the crown. They were never seen wearing ornamental hairpins. Their nature was obedient,

---

"Names of States"

"Massachusetts, Maine, New York, Pennsylvania, New Hampshire, Rhode Island, Connecticut, Kentucky, Ohio, Indiana, Maryland, North Carolina, S. Carolina, Delaware, Mississippi, Illinois." — *Rosenbach Museum & Library*

"Names of States"

"Louisiana, Michigan, Columbia, Florida, Alabama, Wisconsin, Virginia, Georgia, Brunswick, Tennessee. Manjiro wrote the names of 27 out of the 34 states of the United States. He said he had forgotten the rest."

In a footnote Shoryo wrote, "These names of the 34 states have been learned after finishing the study of A,B,C, etc., and 1,2,3, etc., and other basic phonetic spellings, just like teaching Japanese province names to our children. After finishing this, the names of places in the world and the names of the islands were taught. Manjiro said Australia [*Rasshireria*] is regarded as the biggest island. Then it was said they would learn literary expressions gradually, step by step. But as the literary expressions were so difficult to learn from the textbooks at hand, the names of states and islands were actually taught.

"Judging from this experience, Manjiro believes that those who are trying to study a foreign language could learn quicker and more easily by learning the names of places rather than starting the lessons from a textbook, because they will learn the phonetics of combining one letter to another through spelling them. Choosing some names on the map, I wrote Manjiro's pronunciation beside them in katakana. The Chinese translations and other old translations are also added to them. I will be happy if I can be of any help in the making of a map in the Western style of pronunciation." — *Rosenbach Museum & Library*

以上二十七ヶ条

令数三十四列

内ノ地名令其

記スル処如斯

餘ハ已ニ之ヲ忘

却入ト云

"A Map of the United States [Yunaisshiteito] in North America [Nowusu Merike]"

Manjiro's voyages are outlined: In June 1843 he arrived in New Bedford on the *John Howland*. In October 1846 he left New Bedford aboard the whaling bark *Franklin* and returned in September 1849. In November 1849 Manjiro embarked on a seven-month journey aboard the lumber ship *Stiegletz* bound for San Francisco and the California gold fields. — *Rosenbach Museum & Library*

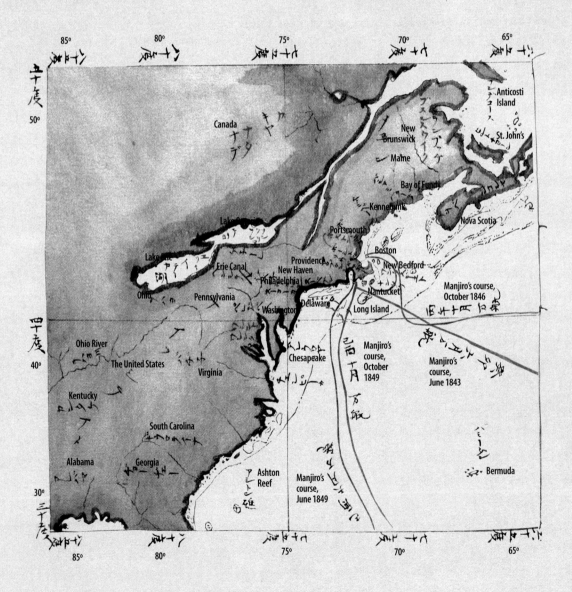

and it had become the custom of the country for women to be highly virtuous. (There were all sorts of people, including those with dark skin, red hair, and a slightly different disposition, probably the results of the blending of different races.)

Food, clothes, houses, and tools were the same as those in Oahu, but Oahu could not compare with Fairhaven in opulence. As in Oahu, people disdained liquor, but those who were idle and permissive would indulge. These people were especially avoided as nobody dared approach them.

Manjiro was now boarded at the house of James Allen for several days. Allen's daughter Jane, who was over 30, taught a number of children at an elementary school in the neighborhood. Miss Allen told Manjiro that if he wanted to learn how to write, she would teach him and bought him a copybook. So he studied earnestly.

Manjiro's Alphabet

Shoryo wrote: "On the right are called the A,B,Cs [*ei-bii-shii*]. They are similar to our country's *iroha* [the Japanese syllabary] and beginning students must learn them. There are about 26 letters. In addition to the three types of writing shown, there are some other variations, but basically no others." — *Rosenbach Museum & Library*

Meanwhile, Captain Whitfield visited a city called New York in the province of New York located 250 miles from Fairhaven. It was the seat of administration[6] for the more than 30 provinces. For their government, people elected a man of wisdom and learning for president who held office for four years. However, if the man were highly virtuous and enlightened, and governed the people eminently, they allowed him to remain in office. The income per year for the president was 1,200 silver pieces. (A silver coin is equivalent to Japanese 2 kan, 500 mon.) Men of talent assembled in the capital from far and wide and competed to be elected to the office. The current president is called Taylor [*Tehera*].[7] He was said to be just in administering punishment, justice, and law. Because the country was governed in such a way, the people would say the United States was better than any other in the world.

In New York, Captain Whitfield visited his brother George and stayed to work on their business affairs. In August the captain brought home his second wife, Albertina, from a place called *Briiji* [Bridgewater]. He then bought farmland on Sconticut Neck, about five miles east of Fairhaven Village, for 1,000 gold pieces and built himself a new house where his wife

6. Manjiro has mistakenly identified New York, the country's largest and most important city, as the nation's capital.
7. Manjiro was not aware that Zachary Taylor died in1850, and his vice president, Millard Fillmore, had succeeded him.

Manjiro's Alphabet and Penmanship

On the page at left, Shoryo wrote: "After learning the A,B,Cs, students learn these numbers. There are also one or two different ways of writing, but generally the above forms are used." At right, he says: "After learning the A,B,Cs and 1,2,3, students learn combined letters which represent intermediate sounds in the alphabet." —*Rosenbach Museum & Library*

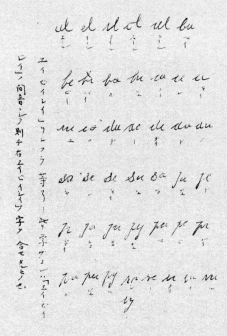

"Floor Plan of the Newly Built House at Sconticut Neck"

This is Captain Whitfield's house on Sconticut Neck, where Manjiro spent about three years growing up. At top, facing west, is the layout of the first floor. From top to bottom, the plan shows the front door, entrance steps, "stove air," and two linen rooms "the size of about 12 tatami mats." Encircling the red-brick chimney at center is a dining room "the size of about 17 tatami mats," a ladder to the upstairs, a rear entrance, and wooden floors. Flanking the dining room on each side are bedrooms. The wing on the east side of the first floor holds a soil room, entry way, and storage rooms.

On the second floor, at bottom, a "wall chimney" at center is encircled by a "sitting area [*shitaya*], the size of about 10 tatami mats," and two bedrooms at right. — *Rosenbach Museum & Library*

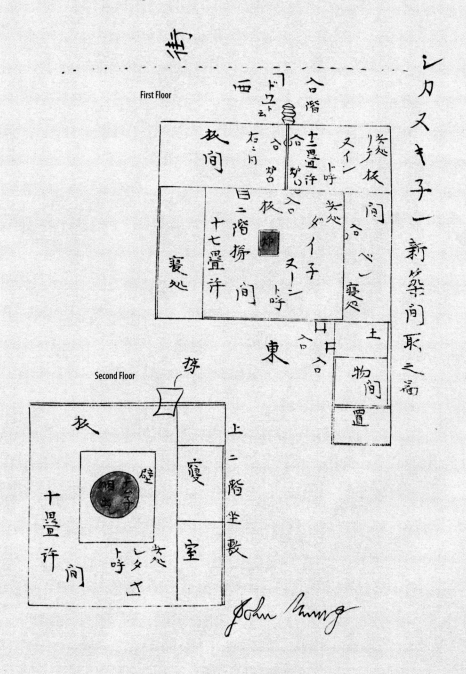

and Manjiro went to live. The family raised cows, horses, pigs, and chickens, and employed some farmhands who sowed corn, wheat, beans, potatoes, pumpkins, melons, and vegetables. Manjiro also helped the farmhands and spent his leisure time each day practicing penmanship. After October and November, when it became severely cold and snow fell, it became impossible to cultivate freely, and Manjiro was able to practice penmanship in the daytime.

In February, the first year of Koka, the Year of the Dragon [1844], Captain Whitfield approached Manjiro and said he should learn reading, writing, arithmetic, and surveying from the scholar Bartlett, a Fairhaven man over 30, who was very learned and talented. Manjiro soon went to Bartlett's school to learn these subjects.[8]

That year, Captain Whitfield and his new wife had a baby boy and named him William Henry. His face was as lovely as a polished jewel. Whitfield's sister, who married a man who had secretly stolen another man's wife and eloped, now lived with Whitfield. She also took care of the newborn baby, for whom her affection increasingly grew. Nevertheless, the child died sometime later while Captain Whitfield was at sea and all the neighbors commiserated and mourned.

In May, the second year of Koka, the Year of the Snake [1845], Manjiro lodged at the house of a New Bedford cooper named Hussey and learned how to make barrels to contain oil. Here he was taken ill and returned to Captain Whitfield's house to receive medical treatment. About that time, the captain was making preparations to go whaling and he asked Manjiro to take care of everything during his absence. In late June, the captain set sail from the harbor.[9]

In February, the third year of Koka, the Year of the Horse [1846], Manjiro recovered from his illness and went to Hussey's once more to lodge and learn the craft of cooperage. In August he returned to Captain Whitfield's house and came upon an old acquaintance, Ira Davis. He was originally from New York and had been a harpooner on the *John James Howland* a few years before, when the Japanese castaways had been rescued. Now he was the captain of the bark *Franklin*, out of New Bedford, and was preparing to go whaling. He immediately employed Manjiro as a crewman. In early October, Manjiro went on board the 168-foot bark.[10]

They set sail from New Bedford with 28 crewmen on board and entered the neighboring port of Boston, considered the finest port in the region. Boston was large and densely settled with more than 100,000 houses. Among the sails and masts of the large numbers of ships

---

8. Manjiro attended the *Louis L. Bartlett School of Mathematics, Surveying, and Navigation* between 1843 and 1846. At the same time, he worked as an apprentice in William H. Hussey's cooper shop on the waterfront.

9. Captain Whitfield actually set sail for the Pacific in the ship *William and Eliza* on October 6, 1844, returning to New Bedford on July 4, 1848, with a respectable cargo of 1,700 barrels of sperm oil.

10. The actual dimensions of the New Bedford bark *Franklin* were: 273.27 tons; length 101 feet 2 inches, breadth 24 feet 6 inches, depth 12 feet 3 inches. Built at Rochester, Massachusetts, in 1822, the *Franklin* was originally smaller and rigged as a brig—with two masts. In the 1830s a consortium of New Bedford owners bought her from the merchant service, had her enlarged and converted to a bark, and put her into the whaling trade, where her career comprised six voyages to the Pacific grounds during 1839-61. Manjiro sailed on the ship's third voyage on May 6, 1846 under Ira Davis. When Captain Davis became ill and had to be put ashore in 1848, first mate Issachar Akin assumed command and, by popular acclaim, Manjiro was promoted to boatsteerer (harpooner). Aikin returned the *Franklin* to New Bedford with a modest cargo of 815 barrels of sperm oil, arriving on September 23, 1849.

Warships at Boston Harbor

On his first American voyage in 1846, at the height of America's war with Mexico, Manjiro sailed as ship's steward on the bark *Franklin*, signing on for a 1/140th share of the ship's profits. The first port of call was Boston, where he sketched warships and fortifications protecting the harbor. Shoryo created these paintings from Manjiro's sketches. — *Rosenbach Museum & Library*

"Waterfront of the City of Boston"

"It is a good 400 or 500 feet tall. Located at the very top of the tower is an object called a weather vane. It is made in the shape of a ship and indicates wind direction by the way it turns. A gigantic clock is placed in the middle of the tower and can be seen clearly from a great distance." Notwithstanding the oriental flavor of the architecture, this is a fine rendition of the Old South Meeting House located at Milk and Washington streets. However, the painting inaccurately places the church on the Boston waterfront. — *Rosenbach Museum & Library*

Boston Harbor

"Weathervanes are installed not only in Boston but they are seen, large or small, in various places." Shoryo's renditions give Boston a distinctive Japanese architectural flavor with their pagoda-like embellishments. *—Rosenbach Museum & Library*

炮臺向背之畾

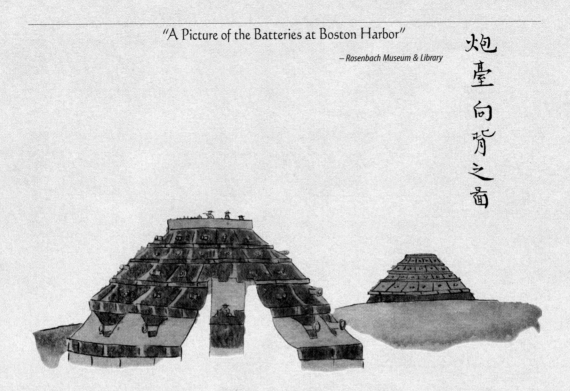

at anchor together, there were numerous huge battleships that had cast anchor there. It was said that the ships were being mobilized for war. A tract of land called Texas sat between the United States and Mexico and both countries claimed ownership. The dispute had turned into war, which had already gone on for three years without either side being victorious.

Both countries had reinforced their arms and fought even more furiously. The battleships were being refurbished to enter the war. Outside the harbor, the men could see several batteries on the shore made of rocks and piled so high they were as tall as buildings—some with four tiers, some with five—and each tier was lined with cannons. These defenses were as forbidding as fortresses. (In the fourth year of Koka, the Year of the Sheep [1847–48], the United States won a great victory over Mexico and finally took possession of Texas.)

After staying in Boston Harbor for three days, they set sail and traveled 2,000 miles, arriving at Fayal Island in the Western [Azores] Islands. Fayal's perimeter was about 70 miles around, and the land had an even climate where many kinds of grains grew. The people looked the same as those of the United States, and their style of clothing was also much alike. After passing the island, the ship sailed on to São Tiago in the Cape Verde Islands, where the natives had dark skin and curly hair. The crew bought some pigs and wood for fuel and continued their journey heading south. When they reached the equator, they headed southeast and rounded the Cape of Good Hope, the southernmost cape of Africa. From there, they headed east, then north, stabbing and catching turtles near an uninhabited island called Amsterdam. The ship headed northeast looking for whales.

"Western [Azores] Islands"

In the fall of 1846, Manjiro's around-the-world whaling voyage aboard the *Franklin* made stops in the Azores, a small group of Portuguese islands in the mid-Atlantic known to mariners as the Western Islands. The ship also stopped at the Cape Verde Islands off the west coast of Africa. These were popular stops where whaleships could sign on crew and buy provisions—at a fraction of the cost they would pay in New England. — *Rosenbach Museum & Library*

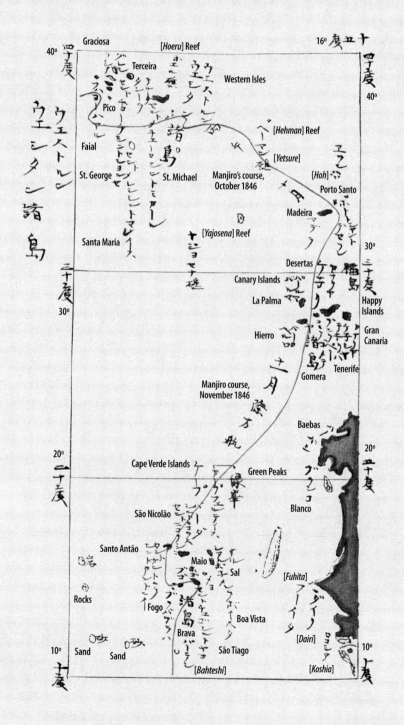

In February 1847, the ship put in at Kupang, in the country of Timor, and stayed there for 30 days. Here were over 200 Chinese-style houses built by carpenters who came from China. The people had black skin and curly hair and were not very small. The country was governed by the Dutch, and their manners closely resembled those of the Dutch. The crew got wood and water and sailed on.

"A Map of Timor Island"

— Rosenbach Museum & Library

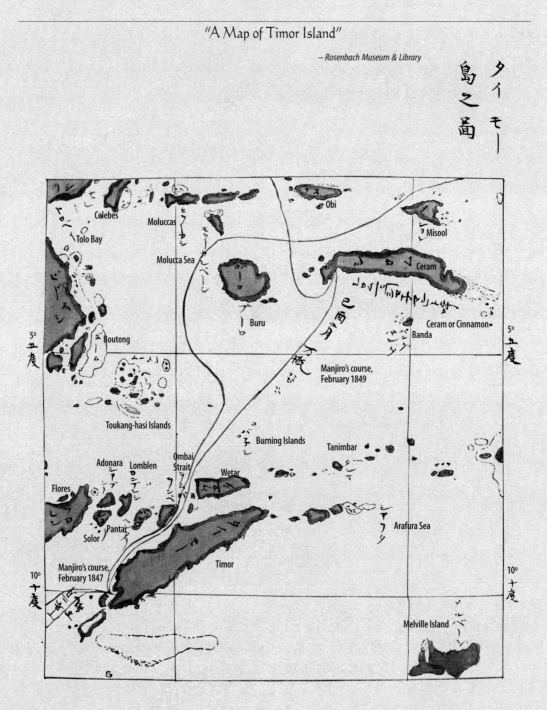

Sailing east along the equator, they stopped at New Ireland. Here it was said that in ancient times the people had deviated from morality and practiced the bad custom of cannibalism. Waiting for foreign vessels, they killed and ate those who were shipwrecked. For that reason, possibly, the natives looked ferocious with their dark-brown skin and tightly curled hair. Both the men and women were tattooed all over their bodies with black ink. After leaving New Ireland the ship rounded the Solomon Islands and caught some whales. Heading north, they reached Guam in March, where they stayed for 30 days.

Leaving Guam, the *Franklin* headed due north and in April reached Bonin (Ogasawara) Island. Until recently this had been a deserted island, but 40 or 50 people from Naked Island and other places had settled there and cultivated several kinds of taro. The crew picked up

---

Natives

The transcriber provided no written information for this painting. — *Rosenbach Museum & Library*

"A Map of New Ireland"

This map traces Manjiro's route aboard the whaling bark *Franklin* as it traversed these islands between February 1847 and November 1848, crisscrossing the equator along the way. — *Rosenbach Museum & Library*

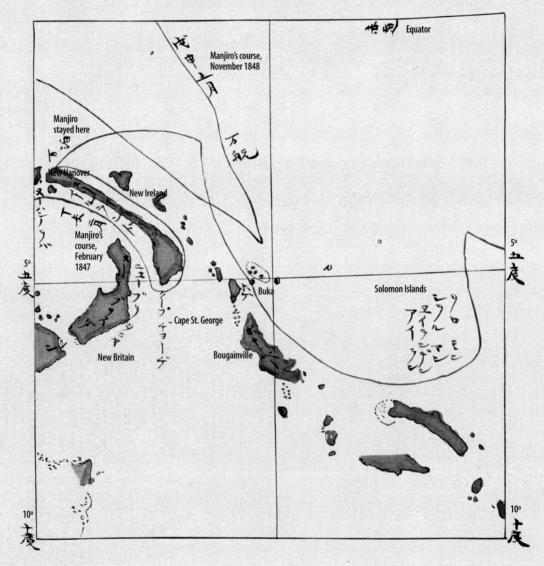

"Ogasawara Islands, A Map of Bonin"

"The circumference of the island is more than 220 miles." Another popular stop for American whaling ships, the Bonin Islands played a pivotal role in Japanese and American negotiations in the mid-nineteenth century. Commodore Matthew C. Perry, during his mission to Japan in 1853-1854, proposed that the Bonin Islands become an open port where American ships, especially whaleships, could be provisioned and serviced. In 1861, the Japanese formed a commission to determine the fate of the islands and dispatched a squadron led by the flagship, *Kanrin-maru,* with Manjiro aboard as interpreter. — *Rosenbach Museum & Library*

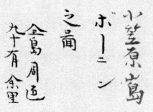

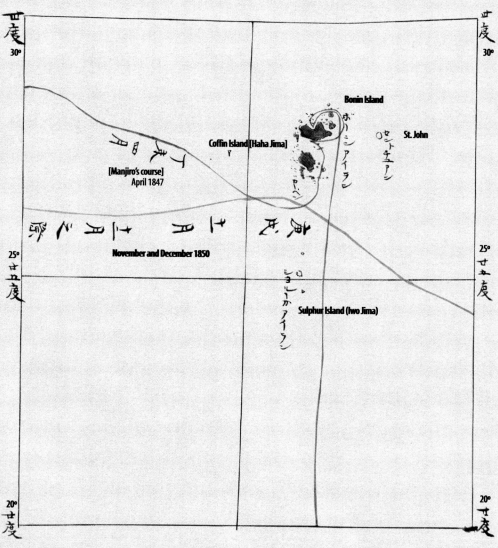

a supply of water from the island and set sail after ten days. In Bonin they heard a story that intrigued and fascinated them. Four years before, a Japanese ship had been wrecked and all but one of the crew had died. The survivor was rescued by a Spanish ship and taken to live there. However, because he was tormented and driven hard in manual labor, he stole a small boat and sailed away. No one knew what had become of him.

Heading due west they arrived at Montgomery in the Loochoo [Ryukyu] Islands. Several men lowered a small boat and landed ashore to do some bartering. They traded two rolls of cotton cloth for two cows. Off again, the ship sailed northeast and reached Japanese waters, where they caught some small fish off the shore of Hurricane Island.

In August, more than 20 small boats were fishing in the open ocean over 480 miles northeast of the island. The crew stopped the ship by furling her sails, then cast out fishing lines. They caught more than 200 bonito. Just then, two of the fishing boats rowed over to the ship. Manjiro put on his Japanese fisherman's clothes, a *donsa*, and tied a towel around his head. Standing at the bow, he called to the men in the boats, asking what province this was. He learned it was Sendai, the province of Mutsu [Miyagi Prefecture].

Manjiro lowered a small boat and took two pails filled with steamed dumplings to the men. He asked them in what direction the province of Tosa [Kochi Prefecture] lay, and the men said they had never heard of it. Though they exchanged further words, they could not make themselves understood to each other. They tried to give Manjiro some bonito but he did not accept them, explaining by gestures that they had caught many bonito a few hours before. With deep bows, the fishermen cordially gave thanks for the dumplings.

Leaving the area, the *Franklin* headed east. In October they reached Sohahho in Oahu and were told that a Japanese man lived there. Soon, Manjiro went to visit him and discovered it was Toraemon. The two friends conversed excitedly about their own circumstances, and each was pleased to see the other was safe and healthy. Toraemon told Manjiro that Fudenojo had changed his name to Denzo, that Jusuke had died in January [1846], and that they had all mourned his death. He went on to say that in October of the same year, Captain Whitfield had arranged for Denzo and Goemon to take passage on a ship to return to Japan. After commiserating about their unfortunate fate in life, they parted.

After returning to the ship, Manjiro heard that a whaling ship had entered port with two Japanese on board. He hurried to visit the ship and found that they were Denzo and Goemon. What a surprise for all of them to see each other after so long! They exchanged salutations about their good health, and Manjiro asked Denzo and Goemon why they had come back. The two brothers wiped their tears as they related the sad story of what had happened in Japanese waters at Hachijo Island and Ezo. They could do nothing but drown in their tears.

Manjiro stayed about 20 days, then bade them farewell. He left Oahu in early November and all looked forward to a reunion one day in Japan. His ship headed due south where they caught some whales off Naked Island, then turned northwest and sailed due west.

In February, the first year of Kaei, the Year of the Monkey [1848], the ship anchored in Guam. At that time, Captain Ira Davis had a mental breakdown and became so violent that the crew bound him in chains. They planned to sail in late April from Guam to Manila, Luzon, and leave the insane captain at the small American office [consulate] in Manila so he could be sent home. Because seamen in many foreign countries navigated and traded around the world, small offices had been set up in various ports to deal with emergencies such as shipwrecks or human problems like that which faced the captain.

Japan did not have such an office, perhaps because of a misunderstanding. A ship from New York once came to Edo and an officer asked permission to station an agent there but he was unable to communicate and the ship returned to America. The Japanese may have feared the captain would report the incident and he would return leading several warships. The story was reported to the Shogunate, and Japan established coastal defenses. When the incident was written up in *The Friend*, an Oahu publication, the author displayed extremely shrewd observations of the Japanese feelings.[11]

When they reached the Luzon Sea, the wind and waves rose so violently that the ship was almost thrown on the sandy shore. The crew had a rough time till, at last, they reached the entrance of Manila Harbor. Manila was a thriving place with beautiful houses standing close together and activity everywhere. The troubled captain was left in another's care, and Akin, the first mate, took his place and managed the ship.[12] In early July the ship set sail from Manila Harbor and caught whales in the neighboring sea. Sailing through the sea off Formosa and the Loochoo [Ryukyu] Islands, they reached Japanese waters and caught whales. In October, they headed south to Guam where they anchored for about 30 days. They set sail again in November and headed south, reaching the equator, where they caught whales in the sea off New Ireland. Then they headed west to the New Guinea Sea.

In February, the second year of Kaei, the Year of the Cock [1849], they landed in Ceram [Suriname], an island country ruled by the Dutch. There were a great many parrots there, and Manjiro bought one to take home and kept it in a cage on board. Arriving in Timor, they bought some chickens, set sail the same day, and headed due west, skirting Bourbon and Mauritius. In May, they passed the Madagascar Sea, rounded the Cape of Good Hope, and headed northwest, bypassing St. Helena.

Finally, in June, they reached the ocean east of North America and in mid-August they returned to New Bedford. Forty months had passed since they had left. They had caught 500 whales and arrived with thousands of barrels of oil. Manjiro received a share of 350 gold pieces [dollars]. When he returned to Captain Whitfield's house, the captain was home and Manjiro eagerly told him of the eventful happenings of his whaling voyage. The captain praised him for his ambition and hard work.[13]

11. In April 1845, the whaleship *Manhattan* of Sag Harbor, New York, visited the port of Uraga at the mouth of Edo Bay and delivered 22 Japanese castaways. It was the first successful contact between an American whaleship and the Japanese authorities. The Japanese representative thanked Captain Mercator Cooper and gave provisions for the ship, but told the captain, in Dutch, to "never come back." Cooper later gave a detailed account of the incident to his friend Dr. C. F. Winslow, in Honolulu. Winslow's story was printed in *The Friend*, February 2, 1846.

12. Issachar H. Akin was 29 years old when he assumed command of the *Franklin*. He is likely the same man as Isaacar H. Akin, who appears on the crew list of the *John Howland*, which rescued the castaways in 1841.

13. The *Franklin* returned to New Bedford on September 23, 1849.

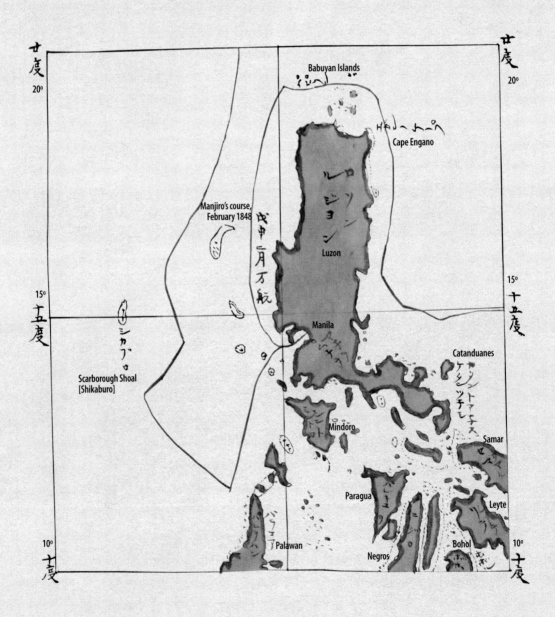

20°

Babuyan Islands

Cape Engano

Manjiro's course,
February 1848

Luzon

15°

Manila

Catanduanes

Scarborough Shoal
[Shikaburo]

Mindoro

Samar

Paragua

Leyte

10°

Palawan

Negros

Bohol

Manjiro was ready for his next adventure. He had heard that in a United States province called California a great gold mine was located within the limits of Sacramento. People who went there from other provinces were at liberty to dig for gold. If he went to California to be a digger, Manjiro thought he would surely get hold of extraordinary wealth and would then be free to do as he pleased. Perhaps he could earn his passage to Japan, which was his dream. He told Captain Whitfield of his intentions and asked for his permission, which was granted. Taking his old acquaintance Terry with him, they took passage on a ship anchored in Fairhaven called *Stieglitz*, which was 130 feet in length. After leaving the port in October, the ship sailed southeast, then turned southwest, rounded Cape Horn and sailed due north.

In April, the third year of Kaei, the Year of the Dog [1850], they reached Valparaiso, Chile, South America, a land that produced gold, silver, copper, iron and several agricultural products. The natives were perfect in build and lived in densely-built houses on the hills behind

---

"South America, A Map of Valparaiso Harbor"

The Stieglitz left New Bedford Harbor on November 27, 1849, and stopped at Valparaiso, Chile, in April 1850 to replenish her stores. The ship arrived at San Francisco on June 21, 1850. — *Rosenbach Museum & Library*

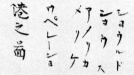

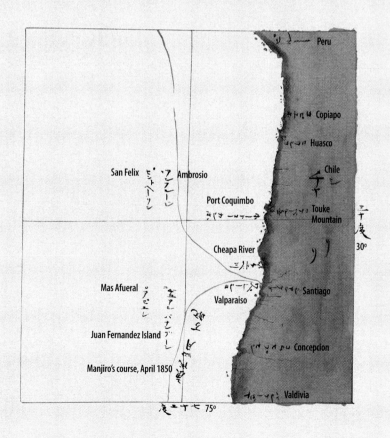

the harbor. Itinerant traders gathered in crowds, which made for lively streets. The *Stieglitz* spent eight days here, then turned north, then northwest, and reached the ocean west of North America.

In late May they reached California and docked in San Francisco. The city sat at the head of a large bay facing an inlet, which was an important resting place for trading vessels. The thriving city was located on the hills behind the bay and over 3,000 closely packed houses lined the streets.

"A Map of Gold mines in California [Kyarefone]"

– Rosenbach Museum & Library

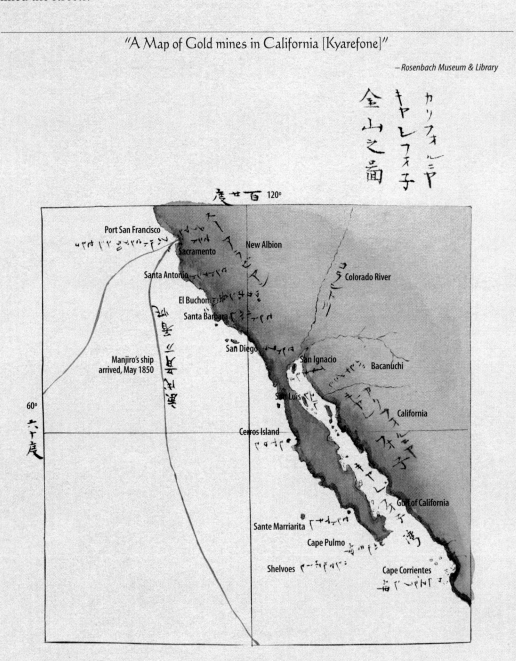

The two companions put up at a hotel for three days and took passage on a strange ship called a steamboat [*schichinbohru*]. More than 240 feet long, it had no sails and was equipped with a huge cauldron in the middle. The iron wheel, which was fixed to the ship on the inside and outside, was turned by use of steam pressure caught from the boiled water, thus propelling the ship. The speed was so great it was beyond comparison. That night they journeyed up a big river for more than 260 miles and reached Sacramento.

After landing, they saw many strange vehicles called railroads [*reiroh*]. (There were very many such vehicles in the United States; Manjiro said he had ridden in one before.)

The railroad ran on coal. An 18-square-foot iron box enclosed a strong coal fire and the accumulated steam was released through an iron pipe. The steam turned the wheels and propelled the massive vehicle at high speed—turning exactly the same way as the wheels of a steamboat. Some 23 or 24 iron boxes were connected in succession. People settled in a box,

"A Picture of a Steamboat [shichinbohru]"

– Rosenbach Museum & Library

"A Picture of a Railroad [Reiroh]"

The twenty-four-car locomotive shown above spans four pages inside *Hyoson Kiryaku*. The primitive renderings of trains on these pages belie Shoryo's familiarity with this technological behemoth. Manjiro, on the other hand, must have been well-acquainted with the iron horse. The Old Colony Railroad was established in New Bedford several years before his arrival in 1843. This great, rolling machine must have been an awesome sight to a young boy, just as it thrills young boys today. — *Rosenbach Museum & Library*

"Railroad, Fire Car"

The watercolor wash paintings on this spread are from the *Hyoson Kiryaku* in the collection of the Kochi Prefectural Museum of History.

put their possessions on the rack above and sat underneath. They could look at the scenery out of windows—three on the right side, three on the left—all fitted with glass. If you looked out the windows, all things slanted sideways; and it ran so fast that nothing remained in sight for long. It was a rare sight. The railroad's path lay where there were no mountains, and iron rods were laid on the ground without a break, for hundreds of miles, so that the railroad could run over them.

They left Sacramento and made their way through rugged territory to the gold mines. For five days they struggled over dangerous terrain, sometimes on horseback, sometimes by palanquin; then they walked over steep, rugged passes impassable for horses and palanquins.

"Steamboats, Fire Ships"

—Kochi Prefectural Museum of History

火船　シテレホール

Hiking for five days, they climbed a high mountain, half-covered with snow, called Sierra Nevada [Eenna]. In the mountains were three big rivers: the North, the South, and the Middle. Gold and silver facilities had been established on the North River by the United States.

When they arrived, they immediately went to work. Manjiro was employed during the day by the gold agency as a miner and was given digging tools. A large pit was excavated and the miners dug there for gold. However, because it was high summer and unbearably hot in the pit, the miners would dig about four feet along the river bank. Gold dust was mixed in the earth and it could be separated from the sand by washing it in the river water. There was said to be a secret to the process. Besides gold, the miners dug for several other metals, such as silver, copper, lead, and tin.

Because of the abundance of gold, the North River area became increasingly more wealthy month after month, year after year. Recently, brothels had opened and miners lined up to go in. The marketplace was filled with stores selling delicacies of all sorts. The place was so prosperous that evil became a product, too. Many people organized in gangs and called themselves vigilantes. Under the pretext of helping the weak, they cheated people out of their money and, in extreme cases, killed them with guns. A great many men were so violent and wayward that the place was ungovernable.

After working for 30 days, Manjiro and his friend received $180 in wages. With the money, they quit the agency and bought their own digging equipment. They put up at a hotel and struck out on their own. If they submitted gold to the gold exchange they often got 20 or 25 silver pieces a day, but sometimes they went empty-handed. Manjiro earned more than $600 dollars in 70 days, an enormous sum of money. He thought it would be indecent to continue. He decided to finish up and go to Oahu, where he would reconnect with his friends, take passage on a ship, and return home to Japan. In early August, Manjiro left the gold mines, traveling back the same way he had come. He boarded a steamboat at Sacramento and arrived at the outskirts of [San Francisco] California.

Seeking passage on a ship to Oahu, Manjiro learned that the *Elisha* from New York, which was twice as large as an average whaling ship, was scheduled to sail. Acting quickly, he paid for passage and shipped out. Heading southwest, the ship reached Oahu in 18 days. Manjiro took lodging at the Konna House and immediately began searching for his friends, Denzo and Goemon.[14]

---

14. The *Elisha* left San Francisco September 17, 1850. The $25 fare was the first time Manjiro paid for an ocean passage.

Book Four

Manjiro urges Denzo and Goemon
to return home to Japan with him,
and the three men begin a final journey.

When Manjiro's ship landed at Oahu in late August, the third year of Kaei, the Year of the Dog [1850], he called on Toraemon first. From him, he learned that Denzo and Goemon lived at Honouliuli, about 12 miles from Honolulu. He immediately visited them, and when the four were together at last he discussed his hope that they would all return home together. Denzo and Goemon agreed, saying they would start making inquiries about passage home. Only Toraemon disagreed, saying that though Denzo and Goemon had previously crossed the sea for thousands of miles and reached Ezo [Hokkaido] and Hachijo, they were unable to return home and landed back in Oahu. It would be best for them to stay permanently in a place they had become accustomed to rather than go through such hardships, perhaps to no avail. Though the other three earnestly tried to persuade him, he was adamant and refused to listen. Nothing could be done. They would have to leave Toraemon behind.

If they reached Japan, they agreed that the Ryukyu Islands to the south would be the most convenient place to land; it would require a small, sturdy boat they could lower from the mother ship and row to shore. Fortunately, Manjiro had a good stock of funds that he had saved from working in the gold mine. He was able to buy a small, solid, well-equipped boat for 125 silver pieces.[1] They were ready to go and, day after day, waited for an opportunity.

In late September, an American ship entered port. The castaways learned there were some Japanese on board and they immediately went to greet the visitors. There were five: Torakichi, age 50, was the captain of the ill-fated *Tenju-maru*, a 90-ton ship from Hidaka, Kii Province [Wakayama Prefecture]; the other four were Kikujiro, 34, Ichijiro, 36, Kichisaburo, 25, and Sazo, 19. Originally there had been 13 men aboard the Edo-bound ship loaded with tangerines and lacquer ware, and they had exchanged these items for 48 tons of rice and several hundred baskets of dried sardines. On their way home the ship had drifted from the Sea of Sagami and experienced difficulties in the ocean to the southwest. They met up with three American ships that came to their rescue. Eight of the rescued sailors were put aboard two ships headed for China. The remaining five men were taken aboard a cargo ship also bound for China.

Hearing the story, Denzo and the others thought this was truly a blessing from heaven. They could go to China together, then go on to Japan. They begged the American captain for passage and he agreed to take them aboard. Torakichi and the others were delighted. The castaways all exchanged accounts of their hardships and an intimacy grew between them. Denzo told them the story of the two castaways, Zensuke from Hyogo and Tobei from Edo, who had previously come to Oahu. He said that he had tried to return with them but was twice refused passage by the captains of the ships those men were on. Now he was pleased that the time was right to fulfill their long-cherished dream.

Hearing the story, Torakichi said that he knew of Zensuke from Hyogo, who was originally from the province of Kii. His family had been members of the samurai in his

---

1. Needing a boat seaworthy enough to carry the three men from ship to shore, Manjiro acquired a used whaleboat, fixed it up, and named it the *Adventurer*.

grandfather's time and later, in Zensuke's day, the family had come to ruin. Zensuke had become a sailor, then a captain of a ship that belonged to a relative of Takadaya Kajuro, a merchant in Hyogo. By about the time Zensuke returned home from his shipwreck, his uncle had died without a successor. Zensuke was adopted by his uncle's family. He inherited the house and was given a fief that would yield 400 bushels of rice. Torakichi had learned all this while he was still in Japan.

Manjiro had learned the cooper's craft while in America, so he was able to repair the broken casks for the crew. However, he got into an argument over wages, which led to a quarrel with crewmembers that made it impossible for him to obtain passage. Because it would be heartless of Denzo and Goemon to leave without Manjiro, they declined passage. Instead, they asked the captain to take care of Torakichi and the others, and they bid farewell. Astonished by this turn of events, Torakichi tried to bring about reconciliation, but his efforts were in vain. Though they remained in port until the middle of October, the ship was finally ready to go. They expressed regret at parting and hoped to meet again some day.

Just then a big ship from Bath, Maine, in North America [the *Sarah Boyd*], entered port and anchored. Manjiro learned it was sailing to Shanghai and had stopped in Oahu to hire crew. He knew the ship's captain, a man named Whitmore, who came from Alabama. Immediately, Manjiro called on him and said they wanted to return home to Japan that year. If the captain would be kind enough to employ them until the ship reached Japanese waters, it would be a blessing.

Though he earnestly begged, the captain was wary, saying it would not be hard to employ a return crew from China—the main problem would be finding crew from Japan to China after the three left the ship. Trying to think of a solution, Manjiro said that neither Denzo nor Goemon were experienced seamen and would not be of much use. But he, Manjiro, would do the duty of both as well as his own. If the captain would be kind enough to take them to the Ryukyu Islands, the two could be dropped off there and Manjiro would go on to China. Furthermore, he would not accept a penny of his wages; his passage would be equivalent to wages. The captain thought it over and Manjiro finally obtained his consent.

Denzo and Goemon kept their plans to return home secret from their friends in Oahu. Their heartfelt wish had not been fulfilled the first time they tried to return home, and they could not be sure things would work out this time. They simply said they would be absent for a while because they were joining the crew on a ship bound for China. Thus, they did not bid their friends farewell. (It was said that Goemon used this trick because he had married, and, though it was inhumane, he wanted to desert his wife.) Manjiro felt sorry that he had not informed Captain Whitfield that he had come to Oahu directly from the gold mines. Now that the agreement had been made, he wrote a letter and said

> I never forgot your benevolence of bringing me up from a small boy to manhood.
> I have done nothing for your kindness till now. Now I am going to return with
> Denzo and Goemon to my country. My wrong doing is not to be excused but I
> believe good will come out of this changing world, and that we will meet again.

The gold and silver I left and also my clothing please use for useful purposes.
My books and stationery please divide among my friends. —John Mung

In his letter he mentioned his possessions in detail. After he dealt with his affairs, he loaded the small boat, his clothing, and other possessions on the ship. In late October, the ship left Oahu Island with a crew of 18 and turned to the northwest, plowing through the waves for more than 30 days.

On January 1, the fourth year of Kaei, the Year of the Boar [1851], they reached 25 degrees north latitude, approaching the Ryukyu Islands. Summoning Manjiro, the captain asked him whether they intended to go as far as China. Manjiro said he would take the two men ashore, then return to the ship and go on to China as agreed. The captain kindly told

---

"Manjiro's Letter to Whitfield"

Although this letter appears in Book Four of *Hyoson Kiryaku*, it is not the one referred to in the text. It's likely that the handwriting is not Manjiro's but belongs to a transcriber. —*Rosenbach Museum & Library*

"Manjiro's Letter to Toraemon"

Although this letter is labeled in *Hyoson Kiryaku* as being the letter sent to Toraemon, it begins similar to one written in March 1847 to Captain Whitfield while he was at sea commanding the whaler *William & Eliza*. At that time, Manjiro was in Guam during his voyage aboard the *Franklin*. That letter begins: "Respected Friend: I will take the pen to write you a few lines and let you know that I am well and hope you were the same." [See the Appendix for the full text of the letter to Captain Whitfield.]

This letter, as well as the one on page 112, is probably written by a transcriber with no knowledge of English. Most of the words are illegible, and the date at the bottom is inaccurate — *Rosenbach Museum & Library*

萬次郎寅右エ門ニ與フル書翰

Manjiro that if his companions were to land then he should also. He would endure a shortage in crew for their sake. Meanwhile, when the ship was about 25 miles off the Ryukyus, they became excited. Though the wind rose from the land, the ship approached a point about seven miles from land around noon the next day. The captain spoke to the three men, urging them to land without anxiety now that the Ryukyus were close.

Manjiro hastily wrote a letter to Toraemon telling him of their situation. He said: "Since we parted in Oahu, the wind has been favorable. Today we are about to land on the Ryukyus. It will not be long now before we return to the home province. Because our journey has been easily accomplished, you should also obtain a passage and return home by all means."

He entrusted the letter to the minister known as Samuel,[2] who had come to Oahu from America. When he bade farewell to the captain and crew, the captain produced a map containing the Ryukyu Islands and showed Manjiro the convenient places to land and where not to land. If they should find it difficult to dock, they should return to the ship. Meanwhile, he would anchor his ship until he was sure they were safe, and only with this knowledge would he depart.

Manjiro thanked him for his kindness, then went to the ship's larder, which was laden with food—mostly cakes and dumplings. Denzo and Goemon had already lowered the small boat and were waiting for him. Manjiro jumped down from the ship and they unfurled the sail. Denzo and Manjiro were at the helm while Goemon pulled the oars, and they headed for the islands. Just then the boat was tossed about on violent wind and waves. Denzo and Goemon were flurried and frightened. Goemon was especially terrified, his legs trembling with fear. He frequently called out to Denzo, afraid that they might be wrecked again, and wondered what to do.

Screaming in fear, Goemon could not hold onto the oar. Manjiro scolded him and furled the sail. Taking the oar from Goemon, he rowed with all his might. Goemon calmed down when they reached the mouth of the bay. Meanwhile, the ship had gone far to the northwest and anchored out of sight. Soon night fell, and they anchored their small boat a few miles off shore. On the third day, Goemon saw people approaching the shore and woke up his two mates. Through weary eyes, tired and sore from several sleepless nights, Denzo looked carefully and saw several figures with fishing rods. Closer to shore, Denzo got out of the boat and approached the people, but they were shocked at the sight of him and ran away. One man turned back and said something. Denzo tried to greet them but could not make himself understood. Returning to the boat, he shouted with frustration that here was another place they could not communicate.

3   The Reverend Samuel Chenery Damon (1815–1885), missionary pastor of the nondenominational Oahu Bethel Church and founder-editor of the widely circulated Christian magazine, *The Seamen's Friend*, was one of the most notable personalities in the Pacific. Actively involved in the religious, social, consular, and political affairs in Honolulu in the 1840s to 1860s, he was also "de facto postmaster," and processed letters not only for Manjiro but also for Herman Melville. Damon took a special interest in Manjiro, writing several articles about him in *The Friend*, and helping him plan his return to Japan. Like Manjiro, Damon traveled to California during the Gold Rush and published a narrative of his journey (1849). He had a chance to see Manjiro in 1860 when the *Kanrin-maru* visited Honolulu on her way back from San Francisco, and again in 1884 when he visited Japan.

However, where there were people there must be houses. Thinking it best to go and visit immediately, Denzo took Manjiro with him and retraced his steps in a search of houses. Because several people came by again, Denzo approached them and asked what the place was called. A decent young man said in Japanese that this was Mabuni-magiri, the province of the Ryukyu Islands. Asked if there were any houses, he answered that there were 30 houses about an eighth-mile from there. The young man asked where they were from and why they were wearing such strange attire. They told him about the shipwreck and said they had been abroad for a long time. The natives gathered around and nodded in understanding, feeling sorry for their weariness.

"A Map of Loochoo (Ryukyu) Islands"

– Rosenbach Museum & Library

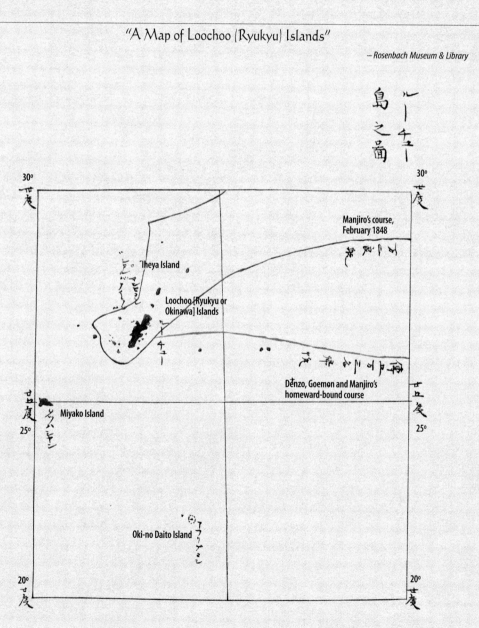

Observing Denzo's exhaustion, a young man from the village put his arm around his shoulder and said he would take care of them and not to trouble themselves. If they went north in their boat for about 120 yards, the beach served as a pier and it would be easy to land there. Denzo left the villagers and went back to the boat. Hoping to satisfy his thirst with tea, he gave Goemon and Manjiro a flask the crew had given them and asked them to get water. When Goemon and Manjiro gestured to the natives that they wanted water, several natives struggled to get the flask first, then visited several houses and dipped for water. The villagers also gave them sweet potatoes and sugar cane in an iron pot. Suddenly, all the households, young and old, came out and stared, wondering at their strange appearance. Those who had previously taken pity on them had also reported them to the government office. More people came to meet them—this time, government officials.

The officials dragged the boat up on the beach and sent all the castaways' clothing and possessions to the office. The three men obeyed so they could get to the office soon and then go home. At the office they were given a small amount of food, such as steamed sweet potatoes. When the officials finished investigating the story of their boat drifting to the southeast and of their many years wandering abroad, they sent a letter to the main office requesting that the men be escorted to Naha, the capital of the Ryukyu Islands, about seven miles away.

"A Picture of a Ryukyu Village"

琉球國
村落之
畧

Though the rain had stopped a short while before, the mud on the road was especially slippery. Denzo's legs ached terribly, and Goemon and Manjiro were so exhausted they found it very hard to walk. They had traveled only a few miles before night fell, but they lit some torches and walked on. About midnight they arrived at a spot about a quarter-mile from Naha. A man loudly calling himself an express messenger from Naha brought word for the party to turn back to a village called Onaga. Finding it harder and harder to walk, they laid some straw mats near the pine trees where the roads crossed. Here they warmed up some gruel to eat and took a nap. At this time, men arrived with bamboo palanquins so they could now be carried.

Heading southwest, they reached Onaga Village and entered what appeared to be a farmhouse, owned by a man named Peichin. Before they had time to make themselves comfortable, a directing official arrived and asked them to follow him, leading them about an eighth-mile northwest from the house. They dragged along, exhausted and hurting, to another farmhouse owned by Peichin's superior. Here several officials met them and investigated the matter of the shipwreck. When they finished giving an account of their travels, it was dawn and the roosters were crowing. They returned to Peichin's house.

Early on the fourth day they were summoned again to the second farmhouse. When they arrived, some officials from Satsuma met them, followed by some spearmen.[3] They asked many questions about the shipwreck and their travels. After the boat was examined, along with their clothing and possessions, they returned to Peichin's house, where they now lodged. Since his house was being used as a government office, Peichin built a straw-thatched house across the street as a temporary dwelling. He moved his wife and eight daughters to the new house; among them were Shiguwa and Ushiguwa.

Sweet potatoes were harvested in the area and so were Japanese banana plants. The fruit was not edible but the women all wove banana fibers into fabric. At the living quarters, five Satsuma officials and two Ryukyu officials worked in shifts of five or seven days guarding the three men. A Ryukyuan cook carefully prepared them meals of rice, pork, chicken, eggs, different kinds of potatoes, bean curd, and fish. At about this time, a messenger from the king of the Ryukyu Islands arrived and gave them some new clothes, including lined and unlined Japanese kimonos and sashes. He also brought them five gallons of distilled spirits. Later, when summer arrived, they were given two mosquito nets.

On July 11, seven high-ranking and low-ranking Satsuma officials arrived on horseback, accompanied by two spearmen. The castaways were told to make preparations because they were going to Naha, so the three quickly put on their new clothes and got into the palanquins. The villagers, with whom they had become acquainted, came and shed tears, and they all expressed regret at parting.

3. The Ryukyu Islands were unified as the Kingdom of Ryukyu in the beginning of the 15th Century. In 1609, it came under the control of Lord Shimazu of Satsuma, who allowed the kingdom to maintain a shadow government in order to continue a relationship with China. Japan asserted full control over the Ryukyu Islands in 1879 and named them Okinawa Prefecture. Mabuni-magiri is currently in Itoman City, Okinawa Prefecture.

At dusk they approached Naha Harbor and boarded an official Satsuma ship, as did the seven officials who guarded them. They loaded the boat and their belongings onto the ship, but it stayed in port for several days waiting for favorable weather. On the 18th of the month the weather was fair and the wind just right, so they left Naha Harbor and sailed for many days toward the province of Satsuma. On the last day of July they entered Yamakawa Port. On August 1, the men were separated, placed on two small boats, and they were off, reaching the harbor at Kagoshima [the capital of Satsuma] at night.

Once ashore, they were detained at the lower meeting place on Nishida Street. Guards came to watch them every day. Under the lord of Satsuma's orders, the officials had to meet the castaways' demands in meals and all other matters, and be kind to them. Daily feasts were prepared as carefully as if for distinguished guests, and they were satiated. Later on, by order of the lord, a suit of clothes and one *ryo* [money] were given to each of them.

In the meantime, a report on the castaways had been submitted to the Shogunate from Satsuma. On September 18, the Shogunate order arrived to send the castaways to Nagasaki,

---

Denzo, age 50, and Goemon, age 28, of Usa, Takaoka County

The two brothers fashion an ensemble of Western attire for their inquisitors. *— Kochi Prefectural Museum of History*

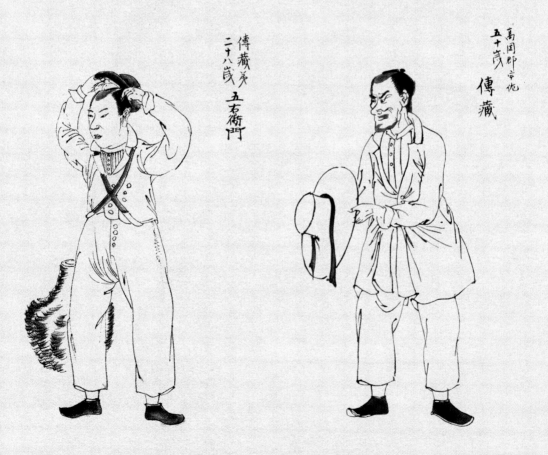

and on the same day the three men left Kagoshima guarded by five spearmen and five officials. They went on foot while their boat and possessions were carried by porters, and on September 22 they arrived at Mukoda. Here, they boarded a river boat and traveled for about 31 miles until they arrived at a place called Kyodomari. Again they transferred, this time to a large ship bedecked with a crested awning of flowing purple silk. Sailing northwest, the ship reached the great harbor of Nagasaki on September 29.

On the morning of October 1, they landed and were taken to the courtyard of the magistrate's office to be interrogated by the authorities. They were asked in detail about the shipwreck. A brass plate about 11 inches square, engraved with human figures, was brought out, and the three were ordered to tread on it. They did as they were told. After Lord Maki Shima-no-kami, magistrate of Nagasaki, inspected them personally, they were detained in a prison on Sakura Street. They were subsequently summoned to the courtyard each day and asked more questions.

Among the implements the castaways had brought back with them was a world map, which Manjiro used to explain where they had been, what the different places were like, and other facts about the world. Finally, the examination was concluded. They were sentenced to three days of imprisonment. Later, they were given Japanese clothes and for the first time their foreheads were shaved in Japanese style.

About this time Torakichi and his companions from Kii, whom they had met in Oahu, were escorted back from China and detained in the prison with them. They were surprised and pleased that they had all returned home safely and had met again unexpectedly. They shared stories about their hardships abroad and wondered what lay ahead.

Fumie

Manjiro's drawing of a Christian medallion depicts two human figures. Manjiro and his companions were ordered to trample on such an object to prove they were not Christians. The practice of stepping on sacred images, called *fumie*, was instituted in 1613 as part of Japan's wholesale prohibition of Christianity. The *fumie* plate usually depicted the Madonna and Child or the Crucifixion." – *Rosenbach Museum & Library*

In March, the fifth year of Kaei, the Year of the Rat [1852], officials from Kii province came to take Torakichi and the others home. They said goodbye to their old friends and promised to meet again later. The three castaways waited eagerly, believing that officials would soon come from their province of Tosa to fetch them.

On June 23 an official named Horibe arrived from their province with 16 others, including an official in charge of maritime affairs and two relatives from the men's families. The castaways were brought before the judges in the courtyard. Lord Maki and other high officials were lined up in the front while Horibe sat by their side. When the maritime official and the three men knelt in the courtyard, Lord Maki said that because they had been able to give a credible account of their shipwreck and had not adopted Christianity, they would be sent back to their home province but would not be allowed to leave again without permission. He added that if they died, someone would have to report it to the authorities. They were also ordered to inform the relatives that Toraemon lived abroad and that Jusuke had died.

"Manjiro, 27 Years Old"

Manjiro dons his wide-brim chapeau and neatly-fitted jacket and pantaloons. Perhaps he's preparing to unfurl the map that will give his interrogators a new look at the world. This portrait, and the portraits on page 119, appear only in the *Hysoson Kiryaku* in the collection of the Kochi Museum. — *Kochi Prefectural Museum of History*

二十七歳
萬治郎

They affixed the fingerprints of their middle fingers under their names in a document. The boat and all its fittings were confiscated, but they were allowed to keep the gold dust, silver coins, coppers, English books, records, guns, powder, foreign dice, and a measuring instrument called an octant. They were given equivalent amounts of Japanese silver in exchange for their gold dust, silver coins and coppers. They left the office and stayed at the Nishikawa Inn, and on June 25, they left Nagasaki.

With favorable weather on land and sea, they reached the border of their native Tosa province on July 9. Passing the checking station of Mochiiguchi, they arrived in the castle town of Kochi on July 11 and were given lodging at the Matsuo Inn near Uramon Street. Daily they were summoned to the courtyard and questioned in detail about the shipwreck and the events that had taken place in their lives abroad. Using Manjiro's maps, the officials questioned them in a similar way as at the Nagasaki court.

On September 24, the examination was finally over. The three men were forbidden to have any occupation related to the sea but were compensated with a life-long stipend and given permission to return to their home village. They joyfully left Kochi on October 1 and reached Usa Village at nightfall.

Denzo's house had crumbled and nobody could tell where its exact location was. They lodged at the house of a cousin named Denzo, who was 45. (The castaway's aunt was married to a man named Denzo; Fudenojo had taken his uncle's name while on Oahu because

---

Denzo, Goemon and Manjiro

Another unique rendering of the three castaways—this one from the Sumiyoshi Shrine—shows the men in kimonos looking casual and at peace. As Denzo fills his *kiseru* (pipe) with tobacco, Manjiro takes notes. — *Sumiyoshi Shrine*

nobody could pronounce his real name. The cousin was also named Denzo after his father.) Relatives and old acquaintances gathered, and there was not a soul among them who did not sob at hearing the long hardships the three had experienced in their lives abroad.

Manjiro left Usa Village early the next day and arrived in Nakanohama on the afternoon of the fifth to find that his old mother was still alive. He greeted his elder brother-in-law Etsusuke (Manjiro's father Etsusuke had died when Manjiro was still small. It was impossible to maintain the household because the children were all small. A villager entered the family as an adopted son and married Manjiro's elder sister Seki, taking the father's name, Etsusuke.) Manjiro was greeted by Seki, Shin, and Tokizo, and his younger brother and sister, Kumakichi and Ume. They all drank in celebration and shed tears on hearing his story of hardships.

The world map that Manjiro had brought back had been carefully selected by an Englishman and newly drawn in 1344 of the Christian era, the third year of Koka.[4] No maps the Japanese used could compare with it in minuteness and perfection. However, because the names of the places had been copied in English and were very difficult to read, the authorities summoned Kawada Koretazu,[5] an artist, to the government office and told him to copy the map afresh and get Manjiro to translate the English words into Japanese for official use.

On October 19, Kawada started to draw. This important project was expected to greatly improve the art of navigation and surveying. By an official consideration, Manjiro was made a hereditary retainer to the lord, and he gratefully received the favor of his country.

---

4. Shoryo erred here. The third year of Koka is 1846.
5. Shoryo refers to himself in the third person. Koretazu is one of his pen names.

嘉永五年歳次壬子冬日草稿畢
半舫齋

"Finished writing on a winter day in the Fifth
Year of Kaei, the Year of the Rat [1852],
by Hanposai [Shoryo pen name]."

123

Epilogue: The Legacy of Manjiro

by Junji Kitadai

I believe good will come out of this changing world.
—John Mung

The *Hyoson Kiryaku* ends with a homecoming and reunion for three of the five shipwrecked fishermen, after an absence of eleven years and ten months. The two brothers, Denzo and Goemon, lived quietly in their native fishing village of Usaura in Tosa Province (today Kochi Prefecture) for the rest of their lives. A third brother, Jusuke, had died of his injuries and was buried in Oahu. Their neighbor, Toraemon, decided to settle in Oahu permanently and his fate is unknown. The Japanese government forbade Denzo and Goemon from making a living as fishermen or talking about their experiences abroad. Such were the rules for returned castaways.

Manjiro's Boyhood Home
Illustration by Masamichi Teraishi, circa 1900. *– Kochi Prefectural Museum of History*

For Manjiro, his homecoming was the beginning of a new odyssey. He enjoyed a long-awaited reunion with his mother, family members and friends in his village of Nakanohama, but it was all too brief. Three days later, he was summoned by the lord of Tosa to return to Kochi to teach English and foreign affairs, based on his experiences abroad. The mission of the school, established by Lord Yamauchi, was to educate young samurai leaders. Manjiro was given the lowest samurai rank of *sadame-komono*. In the rigid class society of feudal Japan in the nineteenth century, it was extraordinary for a lowly fisherman, not even permitted his family name, to be admitted to a fringe of the ruling samurai class.

Just as Manjiro began his new life as a teacher in Kochi, on November 24, 1852, Commodore Matthew C. Perry left Norfolk, Virginia, aboard the *Mississippi* for the Japan expedition. Neither Manjiro nor anyone else could have foreseen that the appearance of Commodore Perry's flotilla of four battleships in Edo (Tokyo) Bay in July of the following year, would shock the Tokugawa Shogunate and put Japan in turmoil. The Japanese called the black-hulled American battleships *kurofune,* or "Black Ships," which became a popular word in the Japanese lexicon and is used today as a synonym for "foreign pressure."

"Delivery of the President's Letter," 1853

— From F. L. Hawks, 1856. Millicent Library

After a 10-day show of force by the giant steam-battleships, the likes of which the Japanese had never seen before, Perry left Edo Bay. He had accomplished his initial mission, conveying a letter from President Fillmore to the the Emperor of Japan demanding that Japan open its doors to the outside world. Perry promised to return for a reply the following year.

Since the early seventeenth century, the Tokugawa Shogunate had issued one decree after another to its people, forbidding contact with foreigners to prevent them from being influenced by Western culture. In this way, a unique system of national isolation was established. In 1612, Christianity was banned and, in 1635, all Japanese nationals were forbidden to travel abroad. Those who went to a foreign country and returned home were executed.[1] In 1641, Nagasaki was designated as a port for foreign trade, and only Dutch and Chinese ships were allowed to enter.[2] A handful of Dutch nationals were permitted to stay in Deshima, a small tract of reclaimed land by the Nagasaki harbor.

Under the policy of seclusion, ordinary Japanese were deprived of news from abroad. Only a small number of political leaders and elite samurai had access to pieces of information brought in periodically by the Dutch and Chinese merchants.[3] Thus in the mid-nineteenth century, leaders of the Shogunate were fairly knowledgeable about the increasing presence of Western powers in the Far East. Their utmost concern, especially after the partial colonization of China by the British after the Opium War of 1840–42, was protecting the integrity of Japan from the threat of Western imperialism.

---

1. In spite of the harsh decree, no records were found indicating that any returned castaways were executed. All the Japanese who were shipwrecked and returned to their homeland were severely interrogated by the authorities, especially about their possible conversion to Christianity but, by the mid-19th century, they were regarded more as the source of new information abroad.
2. On a few occasions, such as when the Dutch colonial administration at Batavia (Jakarta) was unable to send the annual ship to Nagasaki during hostilities with Britain, American ships were chartered as substitutes, sailing with American captains and crews under the Dutch flag.
3. Every incoming Dutch ship to Nagasaki was required to submit a special report to the Shogunate on major affairs abroad, known as *fusetsu-gaki,* which was an important source of information for the Japanese rulers.

Faced with the Black Ships, the Shogunate was at a loss, as the United States was an unknown entity. Occasional contacts were made when American whaleships attempted to approach Japanese ports to hand over Japanese castaways, but they were usually chased away. No one in Japan had a working knowledge of the English language. Commodore Perry's negotiation with the Japanese officials was carried out in Dutch and Chinese.

"Commodore Perry Meeting the Imperial Commissioners at Yokuhama"

– From F. L. Hawks, 1856. Millicent Library

The Shogun sent an order to Lord Yamauchi of Tosa to bring Manjiro to Edo (Tokyo), the capital of the Shogunate, as soon as possible. The fact that it was only eight days after the departure of Commodore Perry demonstrated the urgency of the situation. Manjiro hurriedly went to Edo for the first time. He was now 26.

On an early autumn day in 1853, Manjiro found himself seated in front of the key policy makers of the Tokugawa Shogunate, led by Abe Masahiro, head of the Senior Council of the Shogun (*Roju-shuza*), an equivalent of the prime minister. Unknown to Manjiro, a detailed report of his interrogations by a Shogunate official in Nagasaki two years before had been circulated among the top rulers and Manjiro had been described as "very sagacious and could be useful for the country."

To the inquisitive officials eager to acquire firsthand information about America, Manjiro began to describe its geography and give a brief history of the United States and its political system. This basic knowledge he had learned in Fairhaven, Massachusetts, when he was a teenager. At great risk, he went on to emphasize the unfairness of Japan's isolation policy. Based on his own experience as a whaler, he pointed out occasions of the inhumane and cruel treatment of American whalers in emergency situations at the hands of Japanese officials. He reiterated America's desire to establish friendly relations with Japan and appealed to the country to open a couple of ports for American whaleships.

The extent of Manjiro's knowledge, his serious demeanor, and his straightforward expression seemed to impress Lord Abe and other top officials. Thereafter, he and others often invited Manjiro to talk more about his experiences and observations abroad.

In December 1853 Manjiro was officially appointed as a samurai directly in service to the Shogunate (*jikisan*). As such he was no longer a local samurai of the lowest rank in Kochi but a Shogun's samurai in Edo. At the same time he was allowed to have the surname of Nakahama after the name of his native village. It was unprecedented for a castaway fisherman to become a Shogun's samurai; he was now called Nakahama Manjiro.

One of Lord Abe's lieutenants, Egawa Tarozaemon, grew especially fond of Manjiro and obtained permission from the Shogunate to retain him as his assistant. Egawa, an expert in military science and a progressive thinker, was in charge of building forts on Edo Bay, and he was eager to modernize Japan's defense system, utilizing Manjiro's knowledge of western technology.

On February 13, 1854, Commodore Perry returned to Edo Bay, and this time his menacing

"Napha From The Sea"

Perry's Black Ships lie in wait in Naha Harbor in the Ryukyu Islands, 1853. *— From F. L. Hawks, 1856. Millicent Library*

flotilla was made up of nine warships led by the flagship *Powhatan*. Egawa Tarozaemon volunteered to act as a negotiator with Commodore Perry and asked Lord Abe's permission to use Manjiro as an interpreter. At first, Lord Abe agreed but changed his mind after facing strong opposition from Tokugawa Nariaki, Lord of Mito, an influential relative of the Shogun's family. No one could ignore his opinion.

The Lord of Mito argued that since Manjiro had been saved and educated by the Americans, he would not do anything to disadvantage his rescuers and thus was unfit to act as an interpreter. He even hinted that there might have been an American scheme to plant Manjiro in Japan as a spy, and he advised that Manjiro be kept away from Perry's party and left ignorant of details of the negotiation.

At the same time, the Lord of Mito was well aware of the value of Manjiro, and in his letter to Egawa Tarozaemon, he admonished with a unique metaphor:

> *It will be imprudent, in view of the times, to leave that man [Manjiro] loose at pasture, but to make him too confined and ill at ease would reduce his usefulness. Treat generously, while guarding carefully. There was once a dragon tamed and domesticated that one day drove through wind and cloud in the midst of a hurricane and took flight. Once that man changed his mind and was taken away on an American ship it would be to repent too late.*

After tedious but tension-filled negotiations using Dutch and Chinese to communicate, the Treaty of Amity and Friendship was signed by Hayashi Daigaku-no-kami, Chief Commissioner, and Commodore Perry on March 31, 1854. The treaty provided for the opening of two ports, Shimoda and Hakodate. Japan would treat shipwrecked men humanely and allow foreign ships to buy provisions. Although Manjiro played no official part in the negotiation, his recommendation to the Shogunate was reflected in the treaty that ended Japan's nearly 250-year-old isolation policy.

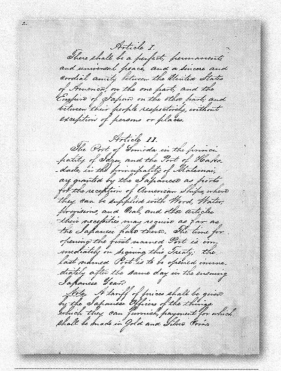

The Treaty of Amity and Friendship

— The Library of Congress / National Archives.

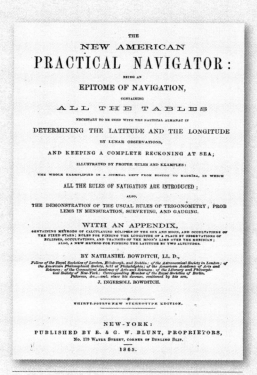

The New American Practical Navigator

— William H. Hegarty Family Collection.

Herman Melville in *Moby Dick,* published in 1851, wrote: "If that double-bolted land, Japan, is ever to become hospitable, it is the whale-ship alone to whom the credit will be due; for already she is on the threshold."

Except for Commodore Perry's "Black Ship diplomacy," Melville's assertion was basically right, but he could not have imagined that a young Japanese castaway, rescued by an American whaleship, would play a historic role.

In addition, Manjiro made many important contributions to his homeland. In 1857, he completed the Japanese translation of Nathaniel Bowditch's *The New American Practical Navigator*, the American seafarers' bible, which he brought back from the United States. It was the first time modern scientific navigation methods were introduced to Japan. In the same year he was appointed professor of navigation at the Shogunate's Naval Training School.

Manjiro became a popular English teacher with eager students, young intellectuals and progressive samurai who had become aware of the importance of learning English rather than Dutch. In 1859, he wrote *Eibei Taiwa Shokei (A Shortcut to Anglo-American Conversation)*, the first English textbook published in Japan. "A Song of ABC" was included.

One of Manjiro's dreams was to introduce Yankee-style whaling to Japan. Based on Manjiro's proposal, the Shogunate decided to sponsor this new enterprise and appointed him to oversee it. In 1859, Manjiro was made captain of the newly built schooner, *Ichiban-maru*, whose first whaling voyage took her near the Bonin Islands. Unfortunately, the ship was badly damaged by a typhoon without making a catch. A few more attempts were made but, to Manjiro's great disappointment, the enterprise never took off. The Shogunate's attention was not focused on whaling but on the domestic turmoil that led to the government's collapse.

In 1858 the Treaty of Commerce was signed between Japan and the United States, and in 1860 officials from the first Japanese embassy brought the ratified treaty to Washington. The principal Japanese delegation sailed aboard the frigate *Powhatan*, courtesy of the U.S. government. Manjiro, in the second delegation, served as an official translator aboard the *Kanrin-maru,* the first Japanese ship that ever crossed the Pacific Ocean to San Francisco.

Among the members of the delegation aboard the *Kanrin-maru* was young Fukuzawa Yukichi, who had learned English from Manjiro. While in San Francisco, Manjiro took him to a bookstore and they bought a few copies of Webster's English dictionary as souvenirs. Fukuzawa later became a fervent publicist of democracy and wrote many books to promote the modernization of Japan. He was the first person to translate the Declaration of Independence and the U.S. Constitution into Japanese. He also founded Keio University, one of the prestigious private universities in Japan. Fukuzawa's portrait is printed on the Japanese 10,000-yen bank note.

Like Fukuzawa, numerous people were influenced by Manjiro directly or indirectly. Perhaps the most famous and popular among the Japanese even today is Sakamoto Ryoma, a young one-time xenophobic nationalist in Kochi. Influenced by Kawada Shoryo, the author of *Hyoson Kiryaku,* he changed his opinion to favor the opening of Japan. Sakamoto's political maneuvering contributed to the collapse of the Tokugawa Shogunate, but he was assassinated a year before the Meiji Restoration of 1868. His proposal advocating a new form of Japanese government with a national assembly was generally attributed to the influence of Manjiro's description of American democracy. Though there are no historical records of personal contacts between Manjiro and Ryoma, it's clear that Ryoma (eight years younger than Manjiro) read the *Hyoson Kiryaku.*

Sakamoto Ryoma

– Kochi Prefectural Museum of History

Sakamoto Ryoma was also known as a founder of Kaientai, Japan's first trading firm, which was short-lived because of his untimely assassination. Mitsubishi was founded as a maritime transportation company by Iwasaki Yataro, a student of Manjiro's in Kochi. The company has grown into one of the leading Japanese business conglomerates and is known all over the world.

Manjiro's influence was large and far-reaching, and his inner life makes for a fascinating exploration. His first odyssey began with the shipwreck and ended with his return to Japan ten years later. It is the story of the amazing growth of a poor, uneducated boy from a fishing village in an insular nation into a stout young man with a sense of mission and an international vision. How did this transformation come about?

Manjiro actually spent more time at sea than on land, first on the *John Howland* before he arrived in New Bedford in 1843; then, in 1846, after acquiring new knowledge and skills, he went whaling aboard the bark *Franklin.* Combined voyages aboard the two whaleships alone lasted for five years and three months. Adding another seven-month voyage around Cape Horn to join the Forty-niners in California, Manjiro spent nearly six years altogether at sea out of his sojourn of ten years abroad.

Manjiro was a contemporary of Herman Melville, and their lives exhibit interesting parallels. On a frigid day in January 1841, just as the 21-year-old Melville sailed from Fairhaven, Massachusetts, as a "green hand" aboard the whaleship *Acushnet,* the 14-year-old Manjiro and four fishermen were drifting aimlessly toward a barren Pacific island—eventually to be rescued by the Fairhaven-commanded whaleship *John Howland.*

The new culture Manjiro encountered and lived in was Yankee whaling culture, as depicted in Melville's *Moby-Dick.* The crew consisted of not only white New Englanders but also people of different ethnic, cultural and religious backgrounds. And "now and then such unaccountable odds and ends of strange nations come up from the unknown nooks and ash-holes of the earth to man these floating outlaws of whalers," as Melville wrote.

In Melville's words, whalers lived in "the long period of a Southern whaling voyage (by far the longest of all voyages now or ever made by man), the peculiar perils of it, and the community of interest prevailing among a company, all of whom, high or low, depend for their profits, not upon fixed wages, but upon their common luck, together with their common vigilance, intrepidity, and hard work."

Moby-Dick's narrator, Ishmael, observed that "a whale-ship was my Yale College and my Harvard." In the same sense, Manjiro was also a graduate of Yale and Harvard on the sea. He was the first Japanese to become an international professional.

Ship *John Howland*

The resemblance of this painting of the *John Howland,* attributed to Caleb Purrington, ca. 1845, to scenes from Russell and Purrington's panorama, *A Whaling Voyage Round the World,* suggests that the ship may be at anchor in Papetoia Bay, Moorea Island. If so, it would have been made from sketches by Russell during his 1841–44 voyage aboard the *Kutusoff.* Waiting out a storm, the *John Howland* (and perhaps the *Kusutoff*) visited Moorea Island with Manjiro aboard in November 1842. *—New Bedford Whaling Museum*

Another important factor in Manjiro's development is his life and schooling in Fairhaven, Massachusetts, from 1843 to 1846, age 16 through 19, his most impressionable years. Under the affectionate protection of Captain Whitfield and his wife Albertina, he received basic education and prepared to be a professional whaler.

Captain Whitfield was a righteous man and an ardent Free-Soiler who opposed the spread of slavery in pre–Civil War America. New Bedford, known as the "Whaling Capital of the World," was a

The Oxford Point School, Fairhaven

Manjiro began his education at this rubblesotne schoolhouse in Oxford Village in 1843. The classroom probably looked much like this 1890s photograph. *—Millicent Library*

hotbed of Abolitionism and became a destination for free blacks and runaway slaves, against whom there was far less discrimination in the whaling industry than in other trades. New Bedforders were also well known for helping slaves on their Undergound Railroad trek to freedom. Yet Manjiro must have felt a taste of racial prejudice when church officials would not allow him to share the Whitfield family pew in a Fairhaven church. Indignant, Captain Whitfield changed his denomination to a Unitarian Church, where Manjiro was accepted.

How religious was Manjiro? This is another fascinating subject yet to be fully explored. He often invoked the name of God in his letters to Captain Whitfield. From Guam, March 12, 1847, Manjiro wrote, "…you are my best friend on the earth, besides the great God. I do hope the Lord bless us whole." Consciously or unconsciously, Manjiro must have been influenced by the humanitarian teachings of the Unitarian Church and by the generally Christian religious atmosphere of a small New England town. But Christianity was banned in Japan, and the Shogunate court in Nagasaki ordered him to do *fumie,* the practice of desecration, which was mandatory for returned castaways. He was forced to tread on a small bronze plate with an image of the Madonna and Child to prove he had not acquired Christian faith while abroad. (Manjiro's last illustration in *Hyoson Kiryaku* represents his *fumie* experience.) The ban on Christianity was not lifted until 1873, five years after the Meiji Restoration.

When Manjiro, 24, returned to Japan, and especially after he became Nakahama Manjiro, a Shogun's samurai, he must have experienced an even more difficult and complex metamorphosis than before. He returned to Japan with the American name John Mung, a whaler and navigator who had literally "seen the world," circumnavigating the seven seas while chasing whales. He had imbibed the Yankee spirit of independence, freedom and rugged individualism. Now, as Nakahama Manjiro, he had to live in the conformity, conventionalism and rigid class consciousness of feudal Japan. As a samurai in the ruling class, he observed a special set of rules in manners and speech which were foreign to him. It was, in a way, a reverse culture shock for Manjiro, who could remember only his poor fisherman's life before he became a castaway.

At least on the surface, he seemed to have adapted to his new life well, but Manjiro must have struggled inwardly with his own identity and the clash of different cultures. One identity was that of John Mung, the free and independent mind; the other was Nakahama Manjiro, the castaway fisherman turned samurai. Moreover, his new celebrity status incited jealousy in conservative circles, and suspicion that he was a foreign spy persisted. When the signing of the treaties with the U.S. triggered a political maelstrom and civil disturbance, nationalist zealots regarded him as a traitor and attempted to kill him. Manjiro was forced to retain a bodyguard to protect himself against assassins.

The *Kanrin-maru*

Painting by Suzufuji Yujiro, a crewmember on the 1860 voyage. – *Yokohama Archives of History*

Manjiro undoubtedly experienced joy when he went back to his home ground in the Pacific Ocean aboard the *Kanrin-maru* in 1860. Soon after the 292-ton bark-rigged corvette left the Japanese coast, it encountered a fierce storm and the Japanese officers and crew, except for Manjiro and a few others, were unable to work because of seasickness and their navigational inexperience on the open sea. Though his official assignment was as an interpreter and he was not responsible for navigation, he was the only Japanese person aboard capable of handling the ship. Without his hard work and the help of American navy officers and sailors who happened to be aboard, it is unlikely that the *Kanrin-maru* could have completed the voyage to San Francisco. The American officer, Lt. John M. Brooke, and his crew of ten were given a return passage to California from Japan on the *Kanrin-maru* in respect for the loss of their ship in a storm near Japan during a survey mission several months earlier.

Lieutenant Brooke recorded in his journal:

> *Old Manjiro was up nearly all night. He enjoys the life, it reminds him of old times. I was amused last night, heard him telling a story...which he followed with a song.*

What Lt. Brooke saw was not the convention-ridden Nakahama Manjiro but the free and unfettered seafarer John Mung at his best. Another entry in the Brooke journal reads:

> *Manjiro is certainly one of the most remarkable men I ever saw....Manjiro is the only Japanese on board who has any idea of what reforms the Japanese Navy requires....*

Manjiro lost his position as the Shogun's samurai when the Tokugawa Shogunate collapsed and the ruling power was restored to the Emperor in 1868 (the Meiji Restoration). The new Meiji Government appointed him as a professor at Kaisei School, the precursor of Tokyo Imperial University.

In 1870 Manjiro was included in a government observer mission to monitor the war between Prussia and France. The mission went to Europe by way of the United States. In New York City, Manjiro managed to take a train and make an overnight visit to Fairhaven to see Captain Whitfield. It was the first reunion in 21 years between the mentor and his protégé; Captain Whitfield was now 65, Manjiro 43. The Captain wrote to his friend Samuel Damon in Honolulu, who had aided Manjiro's return to Japan in 1851: "John Mangero[sic] has made me a visit. He remembers you and all others that befriended him when he was poor. It is wonderful to see the workings of Providence, or the ways of God, to bring about his ends."

Painting of Manjiro, circa 1877

—Dr. Hiroshi Nakahama

In 1871 Manjiro suffered a mild stroke that caused partial paralysis in his lower limbs and a slight speaking deficiency. Though he recovered from his illness in several months, he no longer accepted any public office or job and began to live in quiet retirement.

Japan was rapidly walking the path toward modernization, and many of Manjiro's former students went on to become new leaders in the Meiji government. A new generation of Japanese went abroad to study the affairs of the outside world. Many capable American and European professionals—called "foreign barbarians" by xenophobic nationalists just a few years before—were hired as advisors by the various branches of the Meiji government, bringing merchants and missionaries to Japan.

With information about the outside world becoming more readily available, fewer people sought out Manjiro for advice. It was Manjiro who brought the message of change to Japan, but the messenger seemed to have become obsolete. Or was he?

As Manjiro looked at the enormous changes around him, he must have felt great satisfaction that his self-appointed mission to open Japan to the West was accomplished. At the same time, he must have felt disappointment and loneliness that his message was only half understood, for some of the changes were ominous. In a rush to become a modern nation and catch up with the Western powers, Japan was heading toward a totalitarian military empire. Manjiro's vision of what Japan might be would be realized only after its defeat in World War II, more than a half century later.

"He was like a revolutionary who could not participate in a revolution," wrote Akira Nakahama, in a biography of his grandfather in 1970.

Manjiro had come to possess "revolutionary" ideas, but unlike Sakamoto Ryoma he had no roots in samurai society and power politics in feudal Japan was foreign to him. He was intelligent but could not become an ideologue for a revolution. Unlike Fukuzawa Yukichi, he lacked the basic education in Japanese and Chinese classics required for intellectuals in nineteenth-century Japan.

Manjiro's real message was perhaps born out of his inner struggle between "John Mung" and "Nakahama Manjiro." Out of this unique identity crisis came wisdom and character. His approach to people of all classes and ethnic groups reflected a universal value, equality, and he gave those in different cultures respect and recognition. In this sense, Manjiro's message is very much alive in the world today.

Manjiro married three times after returning to Japan. By the arrangement of his benefactor, Egawa Tarozaemon, he married Tetsu, the daughter of a master swordsman, in 1854. Manjiro, 27, and Tetsu, 17, had a son and two daughters. Tetsu died of measles at the age of 24, and it was said this prompted Manjiro to raise his son to become a medical doctor. Toichiro, the first son, eventually became a prominent physician. Manjiro had two sons in his second marriage and two sons in his third.

Hyoson Kiryaku

The four volumes of *Hyson Kiryaku* from Sumiyoshi Shrine are contained within two books.

On November 12, 1898, at the home of Toichiro in Tokyo, Manjiro started the day with his usual American-style breakfast of bread and his favorite brand of coffee. As regular coffee was scarce, he liked to drink thick Japanese tea with sugar. In the afternoon he suddenly became ill and never recovered. A brain hemorrhage had ended Manjiro's long and eventful journey. He was 71 years old.

In 1976 the National Portrait Gallery of the Smithsonian Institution in Washington, D.C., held a special Bicentennial exhibition, "Abroad in America: Visitors to the New Nation 1776–1914." It featured the portraits of 33 "illustrious visitors" who offered a unique perspective on America. Along with Charles Dickens, Alexis de Tocqueville, Giacomo Puccini, H. G. Wells, and others was John Manjiro—the only Japanese individual. And, as a group, the First Japanese Mission to the United States, of which Manjiro was a member, was also included. At the exhibition, the four volumes of *Hyoson Kiryaku*, borrowed from the Rosenbach Museum and Library in Philadelphia, were exhibited to the American public for the first time.

Manjiro's legacy continues to be felt in the 21st century. The enduring friendship between Manjiro and Captain Whitfield has been nurtured in their descendants. The city of Tosa-Shimizu (which includes Manjiro's home village) and the town of Fairhaven and the city of New Bedford, Massachusetts, signed a sister city treaty in 1987 and are exchanging students and citizens every year. The Japan-America Grassroots Summit, which commemorates the Manjiro-Whitfield friendship, is held alternately in Japan and in the United States every year. Hundreds participate in these fruitful exchanges.

For those of us who ponder the genesis of the relationship between the two nations on both sides of the Pacific, the man we always come back to is Manjiro.

Appendix

1. Letter from Manjiro to Whitfield[1]

Guam, March 12, 1847

Respected Friend

I will take the pen to write you a few lines and let you know that I am well and hope you were the same. First thing I will tell you about the home, the time I left. Well sir your boy, William, is well all the summer but the cold weather sets in he will smart a little cunning creature I ever saw before. He will cry after me just as quick as he would to his mother. Your wife and Amelia and Mr. Bonny's family and your neighborhoods they all well when I last saw them. I did went to Mr. Huzzeys and stayed there about six months and then I left them. Reason is this—they were a good family but very poor living. They only gave us dry hard bread for supper and breakfast and dinner. That's doing well for apprentices, only gave us old Nantucket Dumpling. He have got three apprentices. That is two more besides me. They were left all at once. I was last one in the whole. I thought after them two apprentices left I will stand a better chance, but in vain, so I left too and I was sick in that month three or four times. Then I went to see your wife. Mrs. Whitfield very glad to receive me, so I went to your home and go to the school. After the school out I did try find the place to finish my studies. One gentlemen wished to receive me but the same time United States talks about the war and then I thought make up my mind to go the sea. I went to see Mr. John Howland. He says to me if that I like any kind of a trade he will get it for me. I told him the Bark Franklin the last voyage saw a great many of Japanese fishing boats and the Capt. Ira Davis thought that I might get a chance to reach these; so I shipped for the steward 140th lay. We have caught 30 barrels of sperm oil and have sent it home fifty barrels same last summer we have got in about 50 barrels, 50 bushel apples, 115 bushels potatoes and eight or nine tons of hay, and have sold between three to four tons of hay and we have plenty of milk to drink. I wish you had some of that milk. Your wife is careful and industrious respectful and good woman. I am glad for that you have such good wife. I hope you will forgive me. I hope you never will forget me for I have thought about you day after day. You are my best friend on earth beside the great God. I do hope the Lord helps us whole my friend. Oh my friend, I wanted to see that boy more than little. His cunning little thing I ever saw before. When you get home give my best respects to whole. We were ten months out, sixteenth of this mo. After this we shall go North and Westward toward the Loochue Islands, Japan, and I hope get a chance to go ashore safely. I will try to open a port for purpose for the whaler come there to recruit. We came here to anchor 3rd of this month and saw number of whalers. One of them

---

1. This letter is reprinted from D. R. Bernard, *The Life and Times of John Manjiro*.

touched the Loochue Islands and send the boats ashore in order to see if they can get some of refreshment. Natives gave them two boats and tell go away. One of chief officers says to them in two days if you no sail he cut you float name of this Abram Howland of New Bedford, Capt. Harper. He is going to Japan Sea. He want me to go with him but Capt. Davis he would not let me go. When you see Mr. Warren Woodward give him my best friendly respects. Here I have got letter for you written by your wife. She will tell you more about the home.

John Mung, Japanese

11. Manjiro's Sconticut Neck School

*Report of the Fairhaven School Committee for the year 1843-1844
reviews the facts of District 14: Sconticut Neck District.*

The house in this district is old, and out of repair. It is located in a pleasant place that is, so far as Nature is concerned—but Art has not lent her a helping hand at all. There is hardly any yard room at all; nothing but the street, or the neighbor's grounds, for a play-ground; nothing attractive about it. The house is 18 feet by 25, unpainted, hip-roofed. You know which side is the front, because one side has a door and no window. The entry is 16½ feet by 3½. The school-room is 17 feet by 20, and 9 feet high. It is badly seated. The seats are built up on three sides, the old-fashioned, uncomfortable box seats, all upright backs, and much too high. There is no ventilator, unless a large space where the plastering overhead has tumbled down, serves as one. The room is heated by a close, wood stove. The whole appearance of the room is wanting in neatness and comfort.

There is a black-board, but it has been used the last winter but very little, if any, although the Committee urged the necessity of it upon the teacher again and again. The first time the Committee visited the school, in the winter, he drew an outline map of New England on the black-board, in order to interest the children in that exercise; and at the next visit, more than a month afterward, the same map was there, and not another mark appeared to have been made. Nothing but laziness deprived these children of much knowledge, which they might have acquired by the use of the black-board.

This district has no school library. This fountain of instruction, to them, is dry. They have no school apparatus; and unless they have somebody beside whalemen for teachers, it would be of but little use to have any. But with a teacher who understood his business, and was willing to devote his time to it, school apparatus would do inestimable service.

The whole number of children in this district, between the ages of 4 and 16, is 33…and not half of them attend the school.

III. Japanese Writing Systems[2]

The kana systems, hiragana and katakana, each consist of 46 signs taken from Chinese kanji but strongly simplified over the centuries. Among the syllables are 5 vowels (a, i, u, e, o). The rest are syllables formed by one of these vowels and a consonant (e.g., *ka, ki ku ke ko ra ri ru re ro...*). One exception is *n*. In addition, many syllables can be softened or hardened by adding two small strokes or a small circle in the top right corner next to the character.

Even though one can theoretically write the whole language in hiragana, this system is usually used only for grammatical endings of verbs, nouns, and adjectives, as well as for particles, and several other original Japanese words (in contrast to "loan words" that are written in katakana) that are not written in kanji. Hiragana is the first of all the writing systems taught to Japanese children. Many books for young children are written in hiragana only.

Kanji are ideograms, that is, every character has a meaning and corresponds to a word. By combining characters, more words can be created (e.g., "electricity" in combination with "car" means "train"). There are about 50,000 characters, of which 2,000 to 3,000 are needed for the understanding of newspapers. The government declared a set of 1,945 characters as the "kanji for everyday use."

Japan did not have its own writing system before adapting Chinese characters. In introducing their Chinese characters, the Japanese took over Chinese pronunciation, and associated each character with an existing Japanese word. Consequently, many kanji symbols can be pronounced in several ways, which makes the task of studying them even more complicated.

Calligraphy, the art of writing beautifully, is a popular, traditional hobby in Japan. Most of the Japanese learn it during their school career and continue to practice it as adults.

IV. Calendar[3]

At this time Japan used two calendar methods. One was built upon eras, and changed with either the emperor's reign, the occurrence of great disasters (such as fires, earthquakes, etc.), or *kakunen* (a requirement that the reign be changed in specific cyclical years). During the Tokugawa period, for example, out of a total of 38 *nengo* (eras), 15 were for a change of emperor, 10 for disasters, and 9 for *kakunen.*

In the other calendar system, time and geographical directions were measured using a complex system adopted from the Chinese which used the 12 animals of the Zodiac and five natural elements—fire, earth, trees, gold and water—and incorporated the expressions of Elder Brother and Younger Brother. Time was a

---

1. Information on Japanese writing systems is from the website of *The Pro Team* at http://www.proteamjapan.com/jp_language.htm. The Pro Team is a team of Southern Baptist missionaries working under the International Mission Board through the Japan Baptist Mission.
3. Calendar information and chart compiled by Junya Nagakuni.

flexible entity determined by sunrise and sunset. Whatever the season, the time of sunrise was said to be 6:00AM and the time of sunset was said to be 6:00PM. This lunar/solar calendar, in use through 1872, featured "big months" with 30 days and "small months" with 29. To adjust to the four seasons, an *uruhzuki*, or "leap month," was added every three to five years.

On the traditional lunar-solar Japanese calendar used until the end of 1872, there was *Dai* (30-day) months, and *Sho* (29-day) months. As the moon waxes and wanes in about 29½ days, each month began on the new moon, and the full moon always came on the 15th of the month. To adjust to solar calendar, an *uruh* (intercalary month) was added every two or three years.

The months iterated by the castaways to their interrogators were based on the old Japanese calendar system and have been translated into Western months.

The table below correlates the 12 years the castaways spent abroad to the Japanese calendar system. In the Japanese calendar, there is a period which changes in accordance to the change of the emperors. Accompanying the period is a 10-year cycle of names (*Ye*) based on five natural elements (wood, fire, earth, gold and water) and elder and younger brothers, coupled with a cycle of 12 animals (*To*).

Western Year	Period	Ye (10-year-cycle)	To (12-year-cycle)
1840	11th Year of Tempo	Ka-no-ye (Elder Gold Brother)	Rat
1841	12th Year of Tempo	Ka-no-to (Younger Gold Brother)	Ox
1842	13th Year of Tempo	Mizu-no-ye (Elder Water Brother)	Tiger
1843	14th Year of Tempo	Mizu-no-to (Younger Water Brother)	Rabbit
1844	1st Year of Koka	Ki-no-ye (Elder Wood Brother)	Dragon
1845	2nd Year of Koka	Ki-no-to (Younger Wood Brother)	Snake
1846	3rd Year of Koka	Hi-no-ye (Elder Fire Brother)	Horse
1847	4th Year of Koka	Hi-no-to (Younger Fire Brother)	Sheep
1848	1st Year of Kaei	Tsuchi-no-ye (Elder Earth Brother)	Monkey
1849	2nd Year of Kaei	Tsuchi-no-to (Younger Earth Brother)	Hen
1850	3rd Year of Kaei	Ka-no-ye (Elder Gold Brother)	Dog
1851	4th Year of Kaei	Ka-no-to (Younger Gold Brother)	Boar

Bibliography

Bernard, Donald R. *The Life and Times of John Manjiro*. New York: McGraw-Hill, 1992.

Boss, Judith A., and Joseph D. Thomas. *New Bedford, a Pictorial History*. Norfolk: Donning Co., 1983.

Brooke, John M., and George M. Brooke. *John M. Brooke's Pacific Cruise and Japanese Adventure, 1858-1860*. Honolulu, Hawaii: University of Hawaii Press, 1986.

Fukuzawa, Yukichi, and Eiichi Kiyooka. *Autobiography*. Tokyo,: Hokuseido Press, 1960.

Jansen, Marius B. *Sakamoto Ryoma and the Meiji Restoration*. Princeton: Princeton University Press, 1961.

_____. *The Making of Modern Japan*. Cambridge, Massachusetts and London, England: The Belknap Press of Harvard University Press, 2000.

Kaneko, Hisakazu. Manjiro, *the Man Who Discovered America*. Boston: Houghton Mifflin, 1956.

Kawasumi, Tetsuo, and Shunsuke Tsurumi. *Nakahama Manjiro Shusei (Compilation of Nakahama Manjiro Documents)*. Revised ed. Tokyo: Shogakkan, 2001.

McCabe, Marsha. *A Picture History of Fairhaven*. New Bedford, Mass.: Spinner Publications, 1986.

Meijimura Museum. *John Manjiro: A Bridge between Japan and America*. Exhibition Catalog, October 10, 1992. Tokyo: Nagoya Railroad Company, 1992.

Melville, Herman, Howard Mumford Jones, Harrison Hayford, and Hershel Parker. *Moby-Dick: Or, the Whale*. New York: Norton, 1976.

Millicent Library. *The Presentation of a Samurai Sword, the Gift of Doctor Toichiro Nakahama, of Tokio, Japan, to the Town of Fairhaven, Massachusetts*. Fairhaven, Mass.,: The Millicent library, 1918.

Nagakuni, Junya. *The Sea of Great Ambition : An Illustrated History of John Manjiro*. Kochi Shimbunsha, 1991.

Nakahama, Toichiro. *Nakahama Manjiro Den (Biography of Nakahama Manjiro)*. Tokyo: Fuzanbo, 1936.

Nakahama, Akira. *Nakahama Manjiro No Shogai (Life of Nakahama Manjiro)*. Tokyo: Fuzanbo, 1970.

Nakahama, Hiroshi. *Watashino John Manjiro (My John Manjiro)*. Tokyo: Shogakkan, 1991.

Old Dartmouth Historical Society., and New Bedford Whaling Museum. *New Bedford and Old Dartmouth: A Portrait of a Region's Past: A Bicentennial Exhibition of the Old Dartmouth Historical Society at the Whaling Museum in New Bedford, Dec. 4, 1975-April 18, 1976*. [Dartmouth, Mass.]: Old Dartmouth Historical Society, 1975.

Perry, Matthew Calbraith, Francis L. Hawks, and George Jones. *Narrative of the Expedition of an American Squadron to the China Seas and Japan : Performed in the Years 1852, 1853, and 1854, under the Command of Commodore M. C. Perry, United States Navy, by Order of the Government of the United States. 3 vols*. Washington: A. O. P. Nicholson, printer, 1856.

Plummer, Katherine. *The Shogun's Reluctant Ambassadors, Sea Drifters*. Tokyo: Lotus Press Ltd., 1984.

Rosenbach Museum & Library. *Nakahama Manjiro's Hyosen Kiryaku: A Companion Book: Produced for the Exhibition "Drifting, Nakahama Manjiros Tale of Discovery": An Illustrated Manuscript Recounting Ten Years of Adventure at Sea*. Philadelphia: Rosenbach Museum & Library, 1999.

Starbuck, Alexander. *History of the American Whale Fishery from Its Earliest Inception to the Year 1876*. Washington: Government Printing Office, 1878.

Warinner, Emily V. *Voyager to Destiny; the Amazing Adventures of Manjiro, the Man Who Changed Worlds Twice*. Indianapolis: Bobbs-Merrill, 1956.

Index

Tori Shima Island

Today, the castaways' lonely isle is again uninhabited—though it was not always so. A small poplulation of dwellers were driven away by volcanic eruptions that took place in 1902 and 1939, killing about 125 islanders. The volcano is still active today. – Courtesy of Tosashimizu City, 1992

Nakahama Manjiro

So revered in his hometown, a statue of Manjiro was built upon the green bluffs of Tosashimizu overlooking the blue Pacific to the southeast. — Courtesy of Tosashimizu City, 1992

Caves at Tori Shima Island

Along the southeast coast of the island, cavernous pores formed from spewn lava and erosion provide an inviting shelter for the unassuming castaway. — Courtesy of Tosashimizu City, 1992

Hyoson Kiryaku Maps & Illustrations